YOUR GOLDEN EARS
FIRST
PIANO
LESSONS
FOR ADULT BEGINNERS

ISBN: 978-1-962052-04-7

LEGAL NOTICE

DISCLAIMER NOTICE

YOUR GOLDEN EARS
FIRST PIANO LESSONS

FOR ADULT BEGINNERS

Learn With 5 Minutes Daily Practice, Master Finger Dexterity & Technique Using Sheet Music, Songs, Music Notation and More!

VOL.1

MUSIC MOUSE STUDIOS

Contents

Introduction ix

Your Free Gift! x

Join Our Community! xi

Pacing xii

Keys to Success **1**

Day 1   Piano vs. Keyboard: Making the Right Musical Move!   2

Day 2   Mastering the Piano Layout   6

Day 3   New Note: the Magic of Middle C, Middle C   7

Day 4   Decoding Music Notation   8

Day 5   Understanding Clefs   9

Day 6   Exploring the Rhythm Tree   11

Day 7   Playing Exercise – Putting it All Together   12

The Melodic Prelude **15**

Day 8   Warmup Review   16

Day 9   Decoding Music Notation   17

Day 10   Rhythm Exercise   18

Day 11   Measures, Bar Lines, Intervals, Oh My!   19

Day 12-13   Playing Exercise   20

Day 14-15   Additional Exercise 2   21

Embarking on the Piano Adventure **23**

Day 16   Warmup Review   24

Day 17   New Note E   25

Day 18   Rhythm Exercise   26

Day 19-20   Playing Exercise   27

Day 21-22   New Song: "Mary Had a Little Lamb"   28

Day 23   About Sarah Josepha Hale   29

Day 24   Controversy About the Origins of "Mary Had a Little Lamb"   30

Getting in the Groove   33

Day 25	Warmup Review	34
Day 26	New Note F	35
Day 27	Rhythm Exercise	36
Day 28-29	Playing Exercise	37
Day 30-31	Music Theory	38
Day 32	Dotted Quarter Notes	39
Day 33-35	New Song: "Down the River"	40
Day 36	About Andrea Chang	41

Discovering the Joy   43

Day 37	Warmup Review	44
Day 38	New Note G	44
Day 39	Rhythm Exercises	46
Day 40-41	Playing Exercise 1	47
Day 42	Playing Exercise 2	49
Day 43-46	New Song: "Ode to Joy"	50
Day 47	About Ludwig van Beethoven	51

Silence is Golden   53

Day 48	Warmup	54
Day 49	Rests	54
Day 50	Rest Exercises	56
Day 51	Quarter Rests Exercises	57
Day 52	8th Rests Exercises	58
Day 53	4/4 Time Signature	60
Day 54-57	New Song: "Oh When the Saints Go Marching In"	61

Milky Way Melodies   63

Day 58	Warmup Review	64
Day 59	New Note A	64
Day 60	Rhythm Exercise	66
Day 61-63	New Song: "Twinkle Twinkle Little Star"	67
Day 64	About Jane Taylor	68
Day 65-67	New Song: "The Amazing Twinkle Twinkle Little Star"	69

The Memory Maze   71

Day 68   Introducing… the C Major Scale   72

Day 69   New Note B   74

Day 70   Notes Above B   76

Day 71   Extended Notes of the Scale   77

Day 72   Notes Acronyms: Unlocking Memorization Tips   78

Day 73-76   New Song: "Go Tell Aunt Rhody"   80

Day 77   About Jean-Jacques Rousseau   82

Dual Hand Artistry   83

Day 78   Descending C Major Scale Right Hand   84

Day 79   New Note C in Bass Clef   86

Day 80   New Note B in Bass Clef   89

Day 81-82   Rhythm Exercises   92

Day 83-85   The Grand Staff   93

The Ambidextrous Mastery   95

Day 86   Warmup Review   96

Day 87   New Note G in Bass Clef   96

Day 88   New Note A in Bass Clef   98

Day 89-90   Rhythm Exercises   100

Day 91-94   New Song: "Go Tell Aunt Rhody" (Both Hands)   101

The Power of 3   105

Day 95   C Major Scale Left Hand   106

Day 96   Intervals Review   108

Day 97   Dotted Half Note   110

Day 98   Ties   111

Day 99-101   New Song: "Amazing Grace" – Right Hand   114

Day 102   About John Newton   115

Harmonic Horizons   117

Day 103   C Major Scale Left Hand   118

Day 104   New Note D in Bass Clef   120

Day 105   Chord Structures   122

Day 106-107   Chord Playing Exercises   123

Day 108-109   Chord Playing Exercises   125

Day 110   Music Notation Exercises   128

Day 111-113   New Song: "Amazing Grace" – Left Hand   129

Day 114   Repeat Sign Symbols   131

Day 115-116   New Song: "Amazing Grace" (Multiple Verses)   132

Day 117   Warmup Review   134

Day 118   New Note F in Bass Clef   135

Day 119-120   Name that Note!   137

Leave A 1-Click Review!   139

Conclusion – Beyond the Last Note   141

References   143

Introduction

It was a quiet afternoon as Mrs. Thompson strolled down the streets. Aside from the crisp autumn breeze stirring up the leaves at her feet, the only other thing she could hear was the faint sound of piano music in the distance. Mrs. Thompson quickly recognized the tune, as it was one of her favorite Mozart sonatas. In an instant, she was whisked away to her childhood, where she longed for the moment she could sit by the piano and bring forth enchanting melodies. She had always regretted never taking piano lessons as a child, but life had dealt her the cards it did, and she never had the chance to learn.

Have you ever wished, like Mrs. Thompson, you could turn back time and learn to play the piano? Ever hoped that you could entertain your friends by playing some good old piano classics? Maybe you've always wanted to hone your skills so you could one day play piano at your church. Or perhaps you already are a musician and want to expand your skill set by gaining a solid foundation in piano. Whatever your situation is, it's never too late to start your journey to becoming a pianist!

With this step-by-step comprehensive piano course accompanied by online demonstration videos, you can learn in digestible 5 to 30-minute lessons how to read music from well-known classical piano literature, develop finger dexterity and flexibility, gain a deep understanding of music theory, and uncover fascinating insights about the composers and songs you're learning. Written by a music veteran, Andrea Chang, the founder of Music Mouse Studios, Andrea has a dual B.A. in Music Education and Music Composition from the University of California, Los Angeles, and is an alumni of USC's prestigious Scoring for Motion Pictures and Television program. She also is a graduate of the Conservatory of Recording Arts and Sciences. Andrea has composed music and sound design, and led audio teams for video games for over a decade. She has worked on staff at Electronic Arts, Microsoft, and Hi-Rez Studios.

Taking this first step is a decision that you won't regret! It's an experience filled with challenges, inspiration, and boundless joy that will accompany you for many years to come. But, like any new skill, learning the piano takes time, practice, and patience. If you don't grasp it immediately, don't be discouraged – keep practicing, and you'll get there. If you wish to receive further support, please check out our website www.musicmousestudios.com for additional resources; we have a piano YouTube channel providing demonstrations and options to receive individual support. Thank you for entrusting us with your musical education – we can't wait to walk alongside you on your piano journey!

Your Free Gift!

As a token of appreciation for your support, we would like to offer you a special gift. We have curated a collection of songs and sheet music for you to explore and enjoy, featuring a variety of songs that will further enhance your piano repertoire as you continue your piano journey after the final lesson.

To receive this exclusive free download, simply visit https://www.musicmousestudios.com/contact and include the text "SHEET MUSIC" in your message. We hope these musical gems will bring you joy and inspiration. Thank you for choosing our book!

Join Our Community!

The joy of learning the piano is even greater when shared with a community of like-minded individuals. We would like to invite you to join our piano community, where you can connect with fellow pianists, share your experiences, and receive support along your musical path. Engage in inspiring conversations, exchange tips and techniques, and discover new insights from others who are on the same piano journey as you. Together, we can celebrate achievements, overcome challenges, and foster a sense of camaraderie in our shared passion for music.

To become a part of our community,
visit our website at https://www.musicmousestudios.com/community
and join us today!

Pacing

Each lesson is small, digestible, and designed to be completed within, on average, a 5-30 minute timeframe (though some lessons may take longer). If you need to review a lesson from a previous day, we encourage you to do so – repetition is key to reinforcing and solidifying your understanding of the material. If you already have some musical background, feel free to complete more than one lesson a day. This book is intended to be adaptable to learners starting at various "beginner" levels.

The goal is for each lesson to feel like a one-on-one session with a teacher, so some material will be repeated to help review and build upon the concepts you've learned from previous lessons.

Before diving into each lesson, make sure to scan the QR code below to access the accompanying instructional videos or visit https://www.musicmousestudios.com/ piano-instructional-videos. These videos will provide invaluable guidance and enhance your learning experience. So without further ado, let's get started!

LESSON
1
Keys to Success

Piano vs. Keyboard: Making the Right Musical Move!

A common question that arises is if one should invest in a piano or a keyboard? Each option presents its own unique set of benefits and drawbacks. Let us delve into the realm of keyboards first.

Keyboard

Advantages

1 Price – A keyboard is more affordable if you have a smaller budget. It allows you to gauge your interest before committing to a full-sized piano. Keyboards typically range from $100-$2,000. Though some digital pianos that imitate baby grands can exceed that range, most keyboards lie within those general ballpark prices.

2 Portability and Convenience – Keyboards are smaller and more portable, making it easy to practice at any time or place.

3   Versatility – Most keyboards come with synth patches of other instrument sounds. This introduces you to other instruments and allows you to more easily write your own music, as many keyboards have MIDI capabilities that enable you to plug them into a computer and record the sounds they produce. In contrast, a piano lacks this functionality, and you would need to purchase a microphone and audio interface to record its sounds.

4   Volume control – Many models allow you to adjust the volume up or down or plug in headphones, which is particularly helpful if you're practicing in a location where you can't make much noise.

Disadvantages

1   Finger strength – because keyboards tend to have lighter keys than pianos, often it is difficult for someone who's used to playing solely on the keyboard to transition over to the piano and maintain a consistent, good tone. This generally applies more so to performances. If, for example, you are called to perform your songs on a piano and are only familiar with playing on keyboards, this could be a variable that affects the quality of the performances you give.

2   Technique – While a keyboard can be great for beginners, there may be better options for more advanced players since developing good technique on a keyboard is more challenging. This ties into finger strength but also for more challenging music, such as fast-moving notes or sweeping motions across the piano. These advanced techniques are much more difficult to execute on a keyboard.

3   Overall sound – because the keyboard is an electronic instrument, it won't have the same acoustics as a piano. The piano being a lot larger, has a fuller and more reverberant sound, allowing the pianist to generate a more beautiful tone.

So if you do opt for a keyboard, be sure to choose one with weighted keys, as this will more closely emulate the feel of a piano, helping to build up finger strength and ensuring better control so that you don't accidentally hit a note due to a light touch.

In terms of keyboard brands, a lot of that will come down to personal taste. Yamaha is a solid choice, but I recommend heading to your local instrument store and testing out which keyboard sounds and feels the best to you.

Piano

For those dedicated to playing piano long term, investing in an acoustic piano is the best option. However, acoustic pianos also come at a higher price tag, ranging anywhere from $3,000 to $50,000 or beyond. Similar to keyboards, ultimately, it will also come down to personal preference on the feel and sound of the instrument, but here are some general considerations to keep in mind:

1 Upright versus a Grand Piano

Upright pianos take up less space because they are strung vertically versus horizontally in a grand piano.

Because of that, uprights are also generally less pricey than grand pianos, so if you have a more modest amount of space and budget, I recommend getting an upright piano.

2 The Piano's Sound

Grand pianos are larger and have a fuller sound. If you want that concert experience, a grand piano is the best option. There are baby grands as well as full grands. Baby grands are smaller versions of grand pianos and are usually 5' and 5' 5," compared to full grand pianos that can range from 5' 6" to 9' for a concert grand.

I suggest visiting your local piano dealer to determine which piano's sound you prefer the most. If a baby grand is similarly priced to an upright, I highly recommend selecting the baby grand, as the fuller sound of a grand piano makes a world of difference.

Though many different brands exist, I am particularly fond of Bösendorfer pianos. Consider whether the sound is brighter or darker when trying out and evaluating different pianos. I prefer slightly brighter pianos, but not so bright that they sound like a keyboard. Ideally, you want the sound to be crisp and clear.

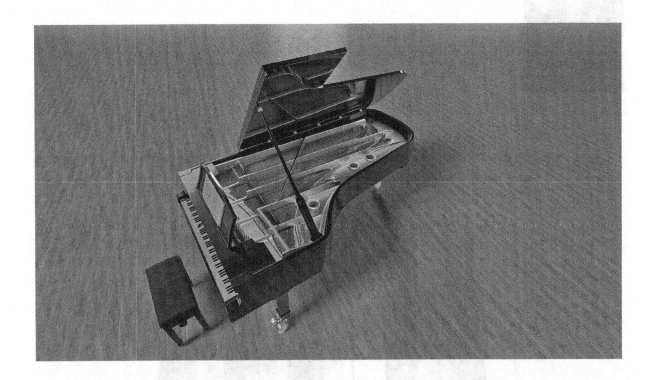

3 The Feel of the Piano

When selecting a piano, it is crucial to assess its sound quality and tactile feel on your fingers, as a piano you can naturally and comfortably play will likely inspire you to practice more frequently. Similar to selecting bowling balls of various weights, pianos also come with keys of different weights. Discovering the ideal key weight that aligns with your preference is essential in finding the piano that brings you the utmost comfort and satisfaction.

DAY 2

Mastering the Piano Layout

A piano consists of white and black keys, and they follow a consistent pattern, alternating between 2 sets of black keys and 3 sets of black keys across the entire piano.

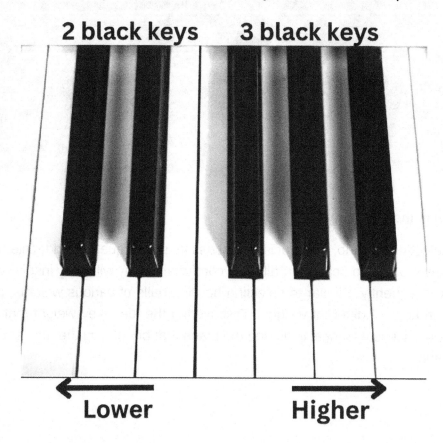

2 black keys   **3 black keys**

← **Lower**   **Higher** →

When you move toward the left side of the piano, the notes get lower. When you move to the right side of the piano, the notes get higher.

Playing Exercise

Video link: *https://www.musicmousestudios.com/piano-instructional-videos*

☐ First, try to play all sets of 2 black keys across the whole piano.

☐ Now see if you can play all of the groups of 3 black keys throughout your piano.

New Note: the Magic of Middle C

C is the first white note underneath the two black notes, as seen in the picture below. We play the note C with our thumbs. Middle C refers to the C positioned right in the middle of the piano. It sounds like this.

Video link: *https://www.musicmousestudios.com/piano-instructional-videos*

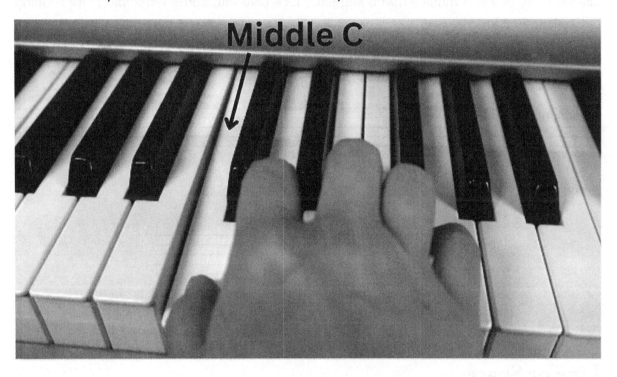

Playing Exercise

☐ Find all the C's on your piano.

☐ Find middle C on your piano.

DAY 4

Decoding Music Notation

When learning a new language, one must master both the written and spoken form. This also applies to music, as it serves as its own language. Learning to read and write music is part of becoming literate and fluent in it. This will create a deeper understanding of what you are playing and make you a better musician who can quickly learn, understand and interpret any piece of music. That being said, let's dive into some terminology for reading and writing music.

As seen below, a staff is what music notes are written on. When counting lines on the staff, we generally count from the bottom up.

Some notes on the staff are on lines while others are on spaces.

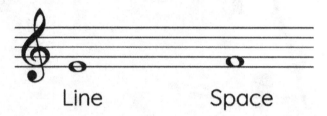

Line   Space

Line or Space

In the exercise below, identify whether the note is on a line or space.

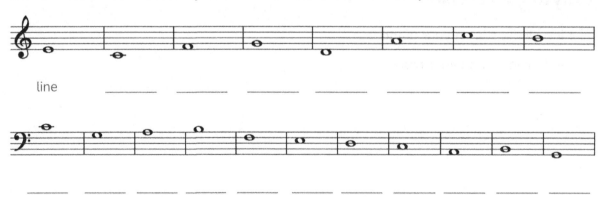

line   _____ _____ _____ _____ _____ _____ _____

_____ _____ _____ _____ _____ _____ _____ _____

Clefs are symbols at the beginning of a staff that show what hand one should play with. As seen below, a Treble Clef signifies to play with our right hand. Notice how the Treble Clef looks like the letter "G," and thus can also be referred to as the "G Clef." Refer to the picture below to see the calligraphy "G's" written next to the Treble Clef.

Treble Clef play with RH

A **Bass Clef**, as pictured below, is placed at the beginning of a staff to signify that we should be playing with our left hand. A Bass Clef looks like an "F"; thus, it can also be called the "F Clef." Refer to the picture below to see the calligraphy "F's" written next to the Bass Clef.

Bass Clef play with LH

First, we will be focusing on just the treble clef. This is what middle C looks like on a treble clef. Notice how it is a line note that is not on the staff but has its own line below the staff. We call this line a **ledger line.**

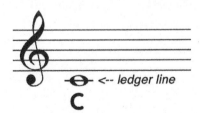

Music Notation Exercise

☐ Draw a treble clef.

☐ Draw middle C.

Within the realm of music, two key elements intertwine: the music notes and the rhythm. We have delved into the music notes, and now it is time to explore the enchanting world of rhythm.

Exploring the Rhythm Tree

Imagine that there is a big fat egg. This egg is 4 beats and is called a whole note. We cut this egg in half, and we get 2 half notes. Half notes are two beats each, with a little stem going upwards from the egg. We take these half notes, cut them further in half, and get quarter notes. Quarter notes are one beat each, and they look like half notes, except the insides of the eggs are filled in. Then we cut the quarter notes in half and get 8th notes. 8th notes are half a beat each and are connected by a little line in between the top of their stems. Staying true to its name, there are eight 8th notes in a whole note, 4 quarter notes (like 4 quarters in a dollar) in a whole note, and 2 half notes in a whole note. Refer to the picture below to see the full rhythm tree.

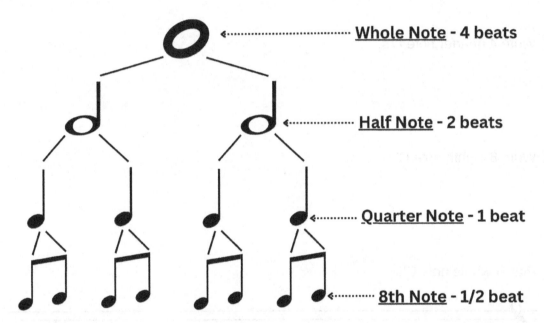

Whole Note - 4 beats

Half Note - 2 beats

Quarter Note - 1 beat

8th Note - 1/2 beat

Note: 8th notes can either be connected like they are above, or they can be single 8th notes. As single 8th notes, they look like this:

8th notes are generally connected together in groupings of 2 or 4 for ease of reading.

Rhythm Exercise

☐ Clap through the rhythm tree for a friend.

Video link: https://www.musicmousestudios.com/piano-instructional-videos

☐ Write 4 whole note C's below.

☐ Write 4 half note C's below.

☐ Write 4 quarter note C's.

☐ Write 8 eighth note C's.

☐ Play 4 whole note C's.

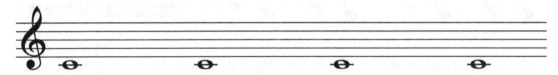

☐ Play 4 half note C's.

☐ Play 4 quarter note C's.

☐ Play 8 eighth note C's.

Video link: *https://www.musicmousestudios.com/piano-instructional-videos*

Congratulations, you've completed Lesson 1!

You are doing an amazing job! Keep going to Lesson 2!!

"Success is not final; failure is not fatal:
It is the courage to continue that counts."

—WINSTON S. CHURCHILL

LESSON
2
The Melodic Prelude

In this lesson, we will deepen our familiarity with the piano keyboard, explore essential music terminology, and enhance our technique through engaging exercises. Get ready to dive in and take your skills to the next level!

DAY 8

Warmup Review

☐ Play all the sets of 2 black notes on the piano.

☐ Play all the sets of 3 black notes on the piano.

☐ Play all C's with your thumb.

☐ Find middle C and play with your thumb.

Notes C-G, New Note D

We play D with our second finger, which is the white note next to C, as seen in the picture below.

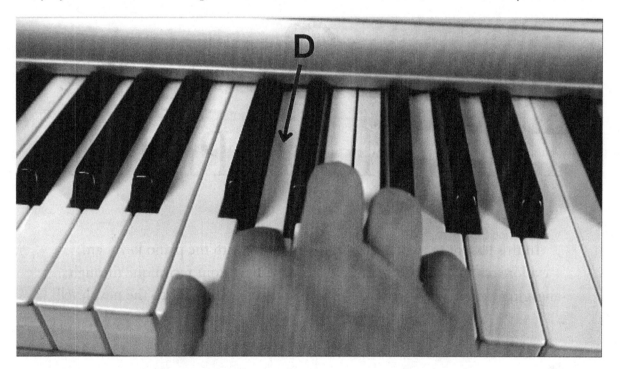

☐ Playing exercise: Play D on your piano.

☐ Playing exercise: Now, let's place all our right hand fingers on the piano. Middle C should be played by your thumb, D by your second finger, E by your third finger, F by your fourth finger, and G by your fifth finger. Play C-G on your piano. Make sure you have the proper hand posture with curved fingers.

Video link: *https://www.musicmousestudios.com/piano-instructional-videos*

Decoding Music Notation

What does D look like on the staff? In the treble clef, D is below the bottom line of the staff on a space note, as seen below.

What does C-G look like on the staff?

In the treble clef, it looks like this:

☐ Music Notation Exercise: Draw a treble clef below and then the notes C to G (like in the example above). Circle D.

Rhythm Exercise

☐ Review: Clap through the full rhythm tree.

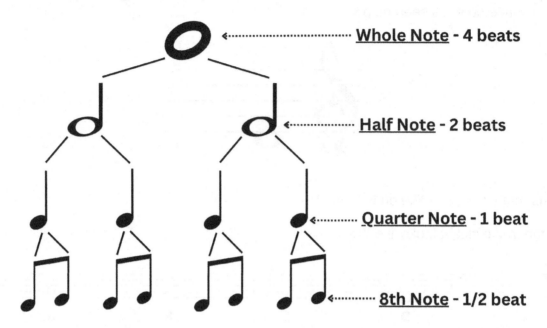

Whole Note - 4 beats

Half Note - 2 beats

Quarter Note - 1 beat

8th Note - 1/2 beat

Measures, Bar Lines, Intervals, Oh My!

Look at the score above. Note that this song has 4 measures. **Measures** are little segments of music broken down by the lines in between the notes. Another name for a measure is a "bar." The lines that separate each of the measures are called **bar lines.**

In the last measure, we see a **chord**, which is when **multiple notes** are played together simultaneously. Chords can consist of any number of notes – 2 notes, 3 notes, 5 notes, etc. Conversely, **intervals** consist of only **2 notes** and are just the number of notes between the bottom and top notes. When the notes are right next to each other on the piano, like how C and D are, this interval is a **2nd** because the number of notes between the bottom and top notes is 2 (C is 1, D is 2). 2nds can occur on any note; for instance, C to D, D to E, E to F, F to G, G to A, A to B, and B to C are all 2nds.

CD
2nd

When an interval is played simultaneously like a chord, it is called a **harmonic interval** since the notes make "harmony" with each other.

In contrast, when the notes in an interval are played successively after each other, we say the interval is arpeggiated or broken and is called a **melodic interval**. The notes are played or sung one at a time like a "melody."

Playing Exercise

☐ Write down the appropriate letters below the music notes.

MEASURE 1   MEASURE 2   MEASURE 3   MEASURE 4

C   CD

Check to see if you got them right below!

C   C   C   C   D   D   D   D   C   D   C   D   CD   CD   CD

☐ Circle all the barlines. How many measures are there?

☐ Clap and count the rhythm. It should sound like the following.

   Video link: https://www.musicmousestudios.com/piano-instructional-videos

☐ Finger the exercise first on the table. For example, the piece starts with 4 C's, so you will hit the table 4 times with your thumb. The following measure has 4 D's, so you will use your pointer and hit the table 4 times. Measure 3 has C, D, C, D, which means you will play your thumb, pointer, thumb, and pointer on the table. The piece ends with 3 chords (CD), which means you will play your thumb and pointer simultaneously 3 times on the table. Make sure you play it to the rhythm of the song.

☐ Refer to the exercise above. Place your thumb on middle C and your second pointer finger on D.

☐ Play this exercise slowly. OPTIONAL: You can speed it up once you have mastered playing it slowly.

Here are some additional exercises to practice.

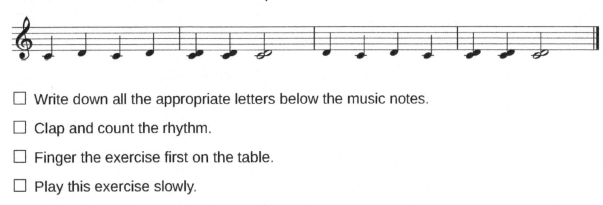

☐ Write down all the appropriate letters below the music notes.

☐ Clap and count the rhythm.

☐ Finger the exercise first on the table.

☐ Play this exercise slowly.

Video link: *https://www.musicmousestudios.com/piano-instructional-videos*

Additional Exercise 3

☐ Write down all the appropriate letters below the music notes.

☐ Clap and count the rhythm.

☐ Finger the exercise first on the table.

☐ Play this exercise slowly.

Video link: *https://www.musicmousestudios.com/piano-instructional-videos*

Congratulations, you've completed Lesson 2!

"To know how much there is to know is the beginning of learning to live."

—DOROTHY WEST

LESSON

3

Embarking on the
Piano Adventure

Let's embark on a piano adventure together as we explore the foundations
of proper hand and finger posture, new notes, music notation, and bring
it all together in a delightful song! Let the musical journey begin!

DAY 16

Warmup Review

☐ Play all C's on the piano with your thumb.

☐ Play all D's on the piano with your 2nd finger.

No Sticky Fingers!

When playing the notes C-G in succession of each other, ensure that your fingers don't keep holding onto any of the previous notes you played. No "sticky fingers"! Focus on allowing each finger to play independently with a good, strong tone. Always practice slowly initially to ensure each finger plays evenly in speed and volume.

☐ Play the notes C through G five times with your right hand, fingers 1-5, respectively. Make sure you have the correct hand posture with the egg underneath, curved fingers, and no sticky fingers!

Video link: https://www.musicmousestudios.com/piano-instructional-videos

New Note E

DAY
17

This week, we will focus on the new note E! E is played in your right hand with your middle or 3rd finger. On the treble clef staff, it is written on the bottom line.

This is where E is on the piano.

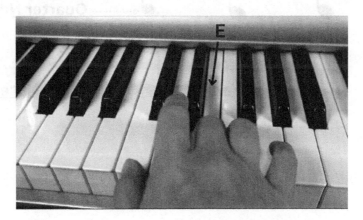

☐ Playing exercise: Find E on your piano.

Video link: https://www.musicmousestudios.com/piano-instructional-videos

Music Notation Exercise

☐ Draw a treble clef.

☐ Draw the notes C to G.

☐ Circle the note E.

Rhythm Exercise

☐ Review: Clap through the full rhythm tree.

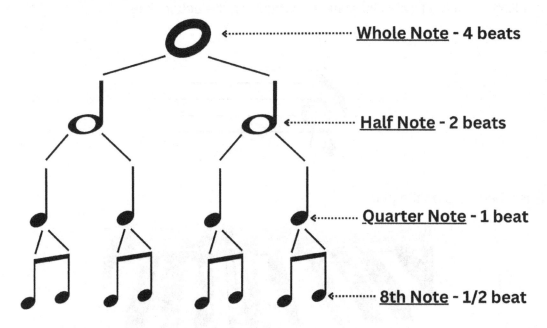

Whole Note - 4 beats

Half Note - 2 beats

Quarter Note - 1 beat

8th Note - 1/2 beat

☐ Look at the score above. Write down all the appropriate letters below the music notes.

In the last measure, when the notes are 3 letters apart (for example, C to D to E), this interval is called a **3rd**.

Answers

C C C   D D D   E E E   C E C E   CE CE CE

☐ Clap and count the rhythm in this exercise.

☐ Finger the song on the table to the rhythm you just clapped (C is played with your thumb, D is with your second finger, and E is with your third finger).

☐ Play this song slowly. OPTIONAL: You can speed it up once you have mastered it.

Video link: https://www.musicmousestudios.com/piano-instructional-videos

DAY 21-22

New Song: "Mary Had a Little Lamb"

We will play your first song – "Mary Had a Little Lamb!" Like the last lesson, remember to follow these steps before playing the music -

☐ Write down all the letters above the music notes.

☐ Clap and count the rhythm.

☐ Finger the exercise first on the table.

☐ Play this song slowly.

Video link: https://www.musicmousestudios.com/piano-instructional-videos

Mary Had a Little Lamb

Words by Sarah Josepha Hale
Traditional Melody

Ma - ry had a li - ttle lamb, li - ttle lamb, li - ttle lamb,

Ma - ry had a li - ttle lamb whose fleece was white as snow.

Check below to make sure you labeled the notes correctly!

Mary Had a Little Lamb

Words by Sarah Josepha Hale
Traditional Melody

E D C D E E E D D D E E E

E D C D E E E C D D E D C

About Sarah Josepha Hale

Born on October 24, 1788, in New Hampshire, Sarah was a renowned writer and editor. She was most well-known for her lyrics to "Mary Had a Little Lamb" and played a pivotal role in establishing Thanksgiving as a celebrated holiday. Some have revered her as the "Godmother of Thanksgiving" because, after the Civil War, she wrote to Abraham Lincoln, urging him to officially dedicate the last Thursday of November as a special day of gratitude to God for the blessings bestowed upon the nation. Lincoln thought this was a good idea and declared that all offices would be closed for National Thanksgiving Day on the last Thursday of November. This marked the beginning of what has become one of our most cherished and widely celebrated holidays annually.

Sarah's education consisted of being homeschooled by her mother and older brother, as well as a lot of self-learning. She went on to become a local school teacher and an acclaimed writer. Sarah was not only the first American *female* writer but the first novelist to tackle the topic of slavery. *Northwood: Life North and South*, published in 1827, was a huge success. In it, Sarah recommended relocating slaves from America to Liberia. She stated that slavery was not only harmful and dehumanizing to the slaves but also to their owners, stunting them both morally and psychologically.

In 1830, she wrote *Poems for Our Children*, which contains *"Mary Had a Little Lamb"* (originally *"Mary's Lamb"*).

☐ Play through "Mary Had a Little Lamb" again.

DAY 24
Controversy About the Origins of "Mary Had a Little Lamb"

This nursery song was allegedly based on an actual girl named Mary, who, in 1815, was assisting her father on the farm when she found a sick newborn lamb. She pleaded with her dad to keep it. Against all odds, Mary nursed the lamb back to health. This lamb followed Mary everywhere she went and indeed had "fleece white as snow." Mary even took the lamb to school one day and hid the lamb beneath her desk under a blanket. When the teacher called her to the front of the class to answer a question, the lamb ran up to follow her. The teacher quickly shooed the lamb out. One of her older classmates, John Roulstone, wrote a poem about what had happened to her that day at school and handed it to Mary. Here was his poem:

Mary had a little lamb;
Its fleece was white as snow;
And everywhere that Mary went,
The lamb was sure to go.

It followed her to school one day,
Which was against the rule;
It made the children laugh and play
To see a lamb at school.

And so the teacher turned it out;
But still it lingered near,
And waited patiently about
Till Mary did appear.

Hale's version contained 3 additional stanzas, and Mary said she didn't know how Hale obtained her poem. Hale claims to have made up *Mary's Lamb.* In the 1920s, after both Mary Sawyer and Sarah Hale had died, Henry Ford, the founder of Ford Motor Company, bought Mary's old schoolhouse and published a book about Mary Sawyer and her lamb!

☐ Perform "Mary Had a Little Lamb" for someone or share it with us on our website, music-mousestudios.com!

Congratulations, you've completed Lesson 3!

"I never dreamed about
success. I worked for it."

—ESTÉE LAUDER

LESSON
4
Getting in the Groove

In this lesson, we will be focusing on some new notes as
well as some groovin' new rhythms! Get ready!!

DAY 25

Warmup Review

☐ Play all C's on the piano with your thumb.

☐ Play all D's on the piano with your 2nd finger.

☐ Play all E's on the piano with your 3rd finger.

☐ Play ascending C D E F G and then descending G F E D C with your right hand.

Repeat this five times. Ensure you have the correct hand posture with the egg underneath, curved fingers, and no sticky fingers!

Video link: *https://www.musicmousestudios.com/piano-instructional-videos*

New Note F

DAY
26

This week, we are highlighting the new note F! F is played in your right hand with your ring or 4th finger. On the staff, it is written on the bottom space.

This is where F is on the piano.

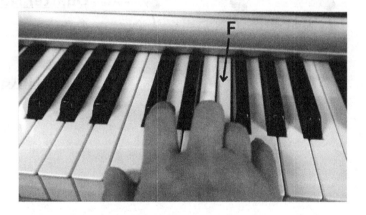

☐ Playing exercise: Find F on your piano.

Video link: *https://www.musicmousestudios.com/piano-instructional-videos*

Music Notation Exercise

☐ Draw a treble clef.

☐ Draw the notes C to G.

☐ Circle the note F.

GETTING IN THE GROOVE   35

DAY 27

Rhythm Exercise

☐ Review: Clap through the full rhythm tree.

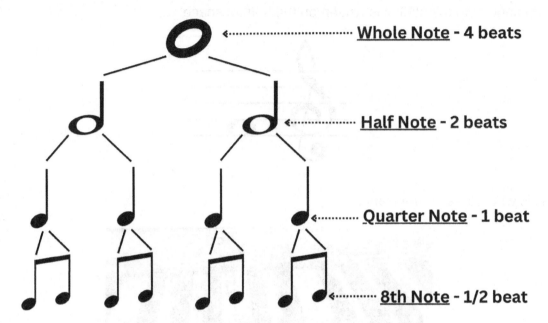

Whole Note - 4 beats

Half Note - 2 beats

Quarter Note - 1 beat

8th Note - 1/2 beat

Playing Exercise

DAY 28-29

Look at the score. Write down all the appropriate letters below the music notes.

Answers below:

C C C C C   D D D D D   E E E E E   F F F F F   C C F F F   CF CF CF

In the last measure, when the notes are 4 letters apart from each other (C to D to E to F), this interval is called a **4th**.

☐ Clap and count the rhythm. It should sound like the following.

   Video link: *https://www.musicmousestudios.com/piano-instructional-videos*

☐ Finger the song on the table to the rhythm you just clapped (C is played with your thumb, D is with your second finger, E is with your third finger, and F is with your fourth finger).

☐ Play this exercise slowly. OPTIONAL: You can speed it up once you have mastered it.

GETTING IN THE GROOVE   37

Music Theory

☐ Look at the score above. Write down all the appropriate letters below the music notes.

☐ Label "2nd" under all the 2nds you see.

☐ Label "3rd" under all the 3rds you see.

☐ Label "4th" under all the 4ths you see.

☐ Check your answers below.

☐ Clap and count the rhythm. It should sound like the following.

Video link: *https://www.musicmousestudios.com/piano-instructional-videos*

Playing Exercise

☐ Finger the song on the table to the rhythm you clapped in the last exercise (C is played with your thumb, D is with your second finger, E is with your third finger, and F is with your fourth finger).

☐ Play this exercise slowly. OPTIONAL: You can speed it up once you have mastered it.

Video link: *https://www.musicmousestudios.com/piano-instructional-videos*

Dotted Quarter Notes

A dotted quarter note is 1.5 beats. This means it's longer than a quarter note but shorter than a half note.

In our rhythm tree, we learned that a quarter note consists of two 8th notes. On the other hand, a dotted quarter note is made up of three 8th notes.

Dotted quarter notes look just like quarter notes but have a dot at the end.

How do we count dotted quarter notes? We count it as "1&2." Think about how you clap a quarter note ("1&") and add another 8th note to it ("2"). Because a dotted quarter note is 1.5 beats, we count one full beat with "1&" and then half a beat with the "2." Refer to the picture below to see how a dotted quarter followed by an 8th note is notated.

1&2 &

The rhythm you are playing for a dotted quarter note is the same as a quarter note plus an 8th note.

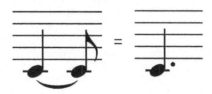

Video link: *https://www.musicmousestudios.com/piano-instructional-videos*

DAY 33-35

New Song: "Down the River"

Down the River

Andrea Chang

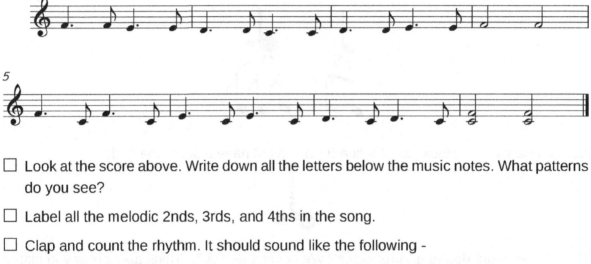

☐ Look at the score above. Write down all the letters below the music notes. What patterns do you see?

☐ Label all the melodic 2nds, 3rds, and 4ths in the song.

☐ Clap and count the rhythm. It should sound like the following -

Video link*: https://www.musicmousestudios.com/piano-instructional-videos*

☐ Finger the song on the table to the rhythm you just clapped (C is played with your thumb, D is with your second finger, E is with your third finger, and F is with your fourth finger).

☐ Play this song slowly. OPTIONAL: You can speed it up once you have mastered it.

About Andrea Chang

Andrea is the author of this book and is a veteran in both the audio and video games/tech industry, where she has worked for over a decade. She has served both as an Audio Director and an Executive Producer at Hi-Rez Studios, a video game company. She built the audio team there from the ground up and has also supervised the centralized audio, art, production and outsourcing teams. Andrea has also provided high-level audio direction as well as hands-on audio support, for all things related to music, sound design, and VO, for all the games and cine-matics at Hi-Rez, such as Rogue Company, Smite, Paladins, Realm Royale, Divine Knockout, and other unannounced games.

Andrea has also worked at Microsoft as an Audio Lead on the HoloLens App, "Actiongram," featuring collaborations with George Takei, Warcraft, Hello Kitty, etc., as well as working as a Senior Sound Designer on the Central Audio Team, supporting audio for company-wide HoloLens and Windows experiences. She sound designed, composed music, implemented audio for augmented and virtual reality across various platforms and devices such as the HoloLens, and VR headsets, among others, and designed audio prototypes to drive inno-vation across the organization.

In addition, Andrea has also worked at Electronic Arts (EA) as an in-house sound designer on their eSports Multiplayer Online Battle Arena game, "Dawngate," as well as having freelanced in the video game and film industry. For a sample of her work, visit www.musicmousestudios.com.

Since covid-19 started, Andrea has homeschooled her daughter. She has detailed her learn-ings, tips, and tricks on successfully juggling working and homeschooling in her book, *A Working Mom's Guide: How to Homeschool Without Losing Your Mind*.

As a content creator, she also enjoys regularly uploading free piano and education resources on her YouTube Channel @homeschoolingwithandrea as well as creating music covers with her daughter. She founded Music Mouse Studios to provide educational and music resources for both kids and adults to help them achieve their dreams.

Perform "Down the River" for someone or share it with us on our website, www.musicmousestudios.com

Congratulations, you've completed Lesson 4!

"Develop success from failures.
Discouragement and failure are two of
the surest stepping stones to success."

—DALE CARNEGIE

LESSON
5
Discovering the Joy

In this lesson, we will be expanding our skillset and learning how to play a famous song called "Ode to Joy" by a well-known composer – Ludwig van Beethoven!

DAY 37 Warmup Review

 **DAY 38** New Note G

☐ Play all the C's on the piano with your thumb.

☐ Play all the D's on the piano with your 2nd finger.

☐ Play all the E's on the piano with your 3rd finger.

☐ Play all the F's on the piano with your 4th finger.

☐ Play the notes C D E F G ascending and then G F E D C descending with your right hand. Repeat this five times. Make sure you have the correct hand posture with the egg underneath, curved fingers, and no sticky fingers!

This week, we will focus on the new note G! G is played in your right hand with your pinky or 5th finger. On the treble clef staff, it is written on the second line.

This is where G is on the piano.

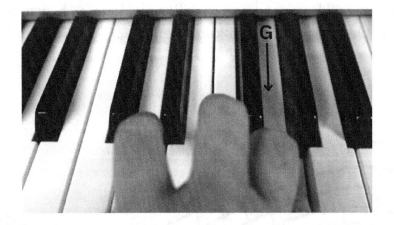

☐ Playing exercise: Find G on your piano.

Video link: https://www.musicmousestudios.com/piano-instructional-videos

Music Notation Exercise

☐ Draw a treble clef.

☐ Draw the notes middle C, D, E, F, and G.

☐ Circle the note G.

DAY 39

Rhythm Exercises

☐ Review: Clap through the full rhythm tree.

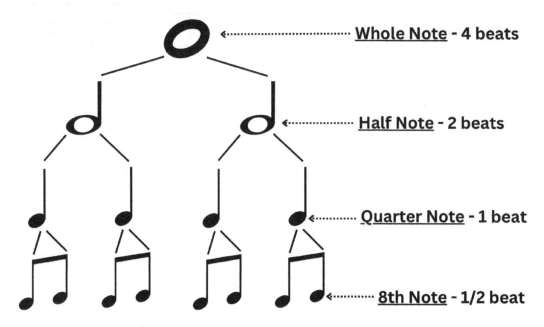

Whole Note - 4 beats

Half Note - 2 beats

Quarter Note - 1 beat

8th Note - 1/2 beat

☐ Practice clapping the rhythm below.

1 & 2 & 3 & 4 &   1 & 2 & 3 & 4 &   1 & 2 & 3 & 4 &   1 & 2 & 3 & 4 &

Playing Exercise 1

DAY
40-41

☐ Look at the score. Write down all the letters below the music notes. The answers are below.

In the last measure, when the notes are 5 letters apart from each other in those chords (i.e., from C to D to E to F to G), this interval is called a **5th**.

Answer

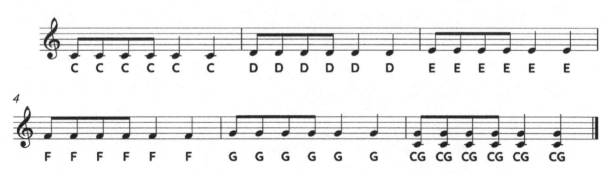

DISCOVERING THE JOY   47

☐ Clap and count the rhythm. It should sound like the following.

Video link: https://www.musicmousestudios.com/piano-instructional-videos

☐ Finger the song on the table to the rhythm you just clapped (C is played with your thumb, D is with your second finger, E is with your third finger, F is with your fourth finger, G is with your fifth finger).

☐ Play this exercise slowly. OPTIONAL: You can speed it up once you have mastered it.

Playing Exercise 2

☐ Find D on the piano.

☐ Play a 5th up starting from D.

☐ Find E on the piano.

☐ Play a 5th up starting from E.

☐ Find F on the piano.

☐ Play a 5th up starting from F.

☐ Find G on the piano.

☐ Play a 5th up starting from G.

☐ Practice playing 5ths beginning on any note on the piano.

Video link: *https://www.musicmousestudios.com/piano-instructional-videos*

New Song: "Ode to Joy"

Ode to Joy

Ludwig van Beethoven

Joy - ful, joy - ful, we a - dore Thee, God of glo - ry, Lord of love;

Hearts un - fold like flow'rs be - fore Thee, Op' - ning to the sun a-bove.

☐ Write down all the letters below the music notes in this song.

☐ What patterns do you see? Do the first and second rows of music look similar?

☐ Clap and count the rhythm. It should sound like the following.

Video link: *https://www.musicmousestudios.com/piano-instructional-videos*

☐ Finger the song on the table to the rhythm you just clapped (C is played with your thumb, D is with your second finger, E is with your third finger, F is with your fourth finger, G is with your fifth finger). Pay special attention to the last measure in each row with a dotted quarter note rhythm. Make sure you feel confident playing the last measure of each row before playing it on the piano.

☐ Play this song slowly. OPTIONAL: You can speed it up once you have mastered it.

About Ludwig van Beethoven

Ludwig van Beethoven, one of the most well-known composers of all time, was born on December 17, 1770, and lived until March 26, 1827. Hailing from Germany, he was a prolific composer despite the profound challenge of losing his hearing at the age of 28. Over the course of 45 remarkable years, Beethoven crafted a colossal body of work, encompassing 722 compositions. Among his magnificent portfolio are 35 piano sonatas, 16 string quartets, 9 symphonies, and a single opera, each a testament to his genius.

In Beethoven's early years, his musical education began under the stern tutelage of his father. Escaping a tumultuous family life plagued by his father's descent into alcoholism, Beethoven found solace with the family of Helene von Breuning. Helene, who he considered his "second mother," educated him and introduced him to the upper social circles. He loved this family and taught their children piano. He also taught piano to the Brunswick family, where he developed intimate connections with the sisters Therese and Josephine Brunsvik. Beethoven harbored an enduring passion for Josephine, but societal constraints prevented their union. Eventually, he encountered Josephine's cousin, Julie "Giulietta" Guicciardi, with whom he had a fervent infatuation as well, which inspired him to compose the renowned "Moonlight Sonata" (Piano Sonata No. 14) in her honor.

In 1784, Beethoven briefly studied with Mozart in Vienna, leaving a memorable impression on the renowned maestro, who declared, "This young man will make a great name for himself in the world." The esteemed composer Haydn, who had mentored Mozart, offered to teach and mentor Beethoven when the prodigy reached the age of 21. Beethoven deeply admired George Frideric Handel and regarded him as "the greatest composer who ever lived."

The year 1814 marked a pivotal moment in Beethoven's life as his hearing loss intensified, ultimately compelling him to retire from performing in public. In a poignant series of letters to his brother, known as the Heiligenstadt Testament, penned in 1802, Beethoven divulged his struggles with deteriorating health and the profound personal loneliness he endured. Despite his seclusion and complete deafness, in this final decade of his life, Beethoven crafted some of his most cherished and revered works, including late piano sonatas, string quartets, and his magnum opus, Symphony No.

9. Notably, the rousing "Ode to Joy" (the song we learned), was a climactic moment within Symphony No. 9, debuted with Beethoven himself conducting completely deaf. He was entirely unaware of the thunderous ovation from the audience cheering behind him until one of the musicians alerted him to the overwhelming response.

Beethoven's life, marked by triumph over adversity and an unwavering dedication to his craft, continues to inspire generations with the enduring power of his music.

Perform "Ode to Joy" for someone or share with us on our website, www.musicmousestudios.com

Congratulations, you've completed Lesson 5!

"When we strive to become better than we are, everything around us becomes better too."

—PAULO COELHO

LESSON
6
Silence is Golden

In this lesson, we will shift our focus to the significance of silence in music
– discover how sometimes the power lies in what we don't play!

DAY 48   Warmup   DAY 49   Rests

☐ Play ascending C D E F G and then descending G F E D C with your right hand. Repeat this five times. Make sure you have the correct hand posture with the egg underneath, curved fingers, and no sticky fingers!

Rests are moments in music when you don't play anything and remain silent. Similar to notes in the rhythm tree, there are also different types of rests as well. Quarter rests, like quarter notes, are 1 beat of silence. Equivalently, half rests are 2 beats of silence, and 8th rests are half a beat of silence. A half rest looks like a hat; conversely, a whole rest looks like an upside-down hat. A quarter rest looks like a squiggly "3," while an 8th rest looks like a little fancy "7."

Take a look at the rests tree below and familiarize yourself with it.

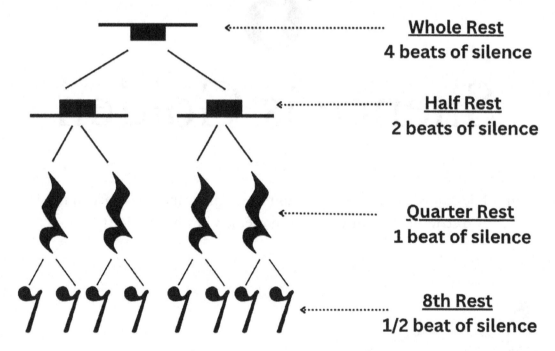

Whole Rest
4 beats of silence

Half Rest
2 beats of silence

Quarter Rest
1 beat of silence

8th Rest
1/2 beat of silence

Video link: https://www.musicmousestudios.com/piano-instructional-videos

Music Notation

A whole rest, half rest, quarter rest, and 8th rest are respectively seen above. On the staff, counting from the bottom line up, the whole rest hangs below the 4th line. The half rest sits on top of the 3rd line, while the quarter rest is between the staff's bottom and top lines. The 8th rests are smaller, so they sit between the 2nd and 4th lines of the staff.

Music Notation Exercise

☐ Use the staff above to draw a whole rest.

☐ Use the staff above to draw a half rest.

☐ Use the staff above to draw a quarter rest.

☐ Use the staff above to draw an eighth rest.

DAY 50

Rest Exercises

Half Rests Exercises

Let's take a look at some half rests exercises. Clap the exercises below. Remember that on the rests, you don't clap (for example, in Exercise 1, don't clap on beats 3 and 4).

Video link: https://www.musicmousestudios.com/piano-instructional-videos

Exercise 1

1 2 3 4

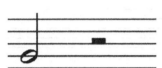

Exercise 2

1 2 3 4

Exercise 3

1 2 3 4

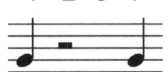

Exercise 4

1 2 3 4

Can you play all 4 Half Rests Exercises together? Give it a try slowly!

1 2 3 4   1 2 3 4   1 2 3 4   1 2 3 4

Quarter Rests Exercises

DAY 51

Let's take a look at some quarter rests exercises. Clap Exercise 1 below – remember that on the rests, you don't clap (for example, in Exercise 1, don't clap on beats 2 and 4).

Video link: https://www.musicmousestudios.com/piano-instructional-videos

Exercise 1

Exercise 2

Exercise 3

Exercise 4

Can you play all 4 Quarter Rest Exercises together? Try it out!

SILENCE IS GOLDEN

8th Rests Exercises

Let's take a look at some 8th rests exercises. Clap Exercise 1 below – remember that on the rests, you don't clap (for example, in Exercise 1, don't clap on the &'s of every beat).

Video link: https://www.musicmousestudios.com/piano-instructional-videos

Exercise 1

Exercise 2

Exercise 3

Exercise 4

Can you play all four 8th Rest Exercises together? You can do it! ☺

Whole Rests Exercises

Whole rests are straightforward – you don't play anything for 4 beats! Give it a try below.

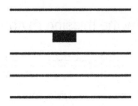

DAY 53

$\frac{4}{4}$ Time Signature

At the beginning of every staff, we have a clef and then a time signature. A time signature tells us how many beats are in a measure and the unit of measurement for a beat. In 4/4, the top 4 tells us that there are 4 beats in a measure, and the bottom 4 tells us that the quarter note gets 1 beat. All of the songs we have played this far have been in 4/4, but later pieces will have other time signatures, which not only will have different numbers in them, but the music will also have a different feel. In 4/4, beats 1 and 3 will feel stronger, and beats 2 and 4 will feel weaker.

 # beats per measure
There are 4 beats per a measure
What note gets 1 beat?
When 4's on the bottom, quarter gets 1 beat

Fill in the Beats!

☐ To complete each measure, draw the missing rhythm note(s) on the note G.

☐ Check your answers below.

☐ Draw the missing rhythm note(s) on the note G.

☐ Check your answers below.

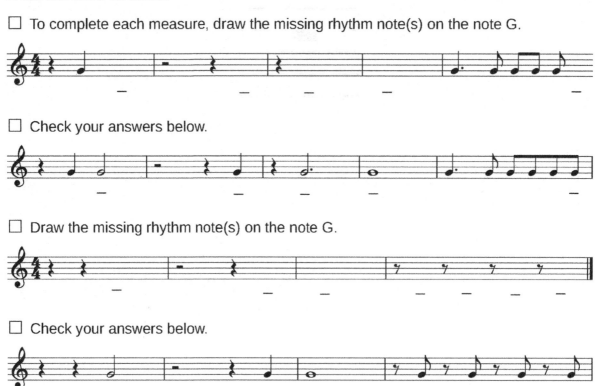

Oh When the Saints Go Marching In

Traditional

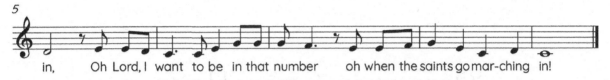

☐ Write down all the letters for "Oh When the Saints Go Marching In."

☐ Clap and count the rhythm. It should sound like the following -

Video link: https://www.musicmousestudios.com/piano-instructional-videos

Pay special attention to measure 7, which has a rhythm that's a bit trickier. You might want to practice clapping this measure individually a couple of times first.

☐ Finger the song on the table to the rhythm you just clapped (C is played with your thumb, D is with your second finger, E is with your third finger, F is with your fourth finger, G is with your fifth finger).

☐ Play this song slowly. OPTIONAL: You can speed it up once you have mastered it.

Congratulations, you've completed Lesson 6!

"Opportunity is missed by most people because it is dressed in overalls and looks like work."

—THOMAS EDISON

LESSON
7
Milky Way Melodies

In this lesson, we will be learning a beloved and recognizable song. Get ready to embark on a musical journey that will bring the celestial wonders to life at your fingertips!

☐ Play ascending C D E F G and then descending G F E D C with your right hand. Repeat this five times. Make sure you have the correct hand posture with the egg underneath, curved fingers, and no sticky fingers!

☐ Find middle C with your left hand. Go to the C below this with your pinky in your left hand. Now place your 4th finger on this D (below middle C), 3rd finger on this E (below middle C), 2nd finger on F (below middle C), and thumb on G (below middle C). These are the same notes (C D E F G) but with your left hand.

☐ Play C D E F G (all these notes below middle C) ascending and descending with your left hand 5 times. Practice slowly to ensure no sticky fingers!

This week, we will focus on the new note A! A is the note next to G. On the staff, it is written in the second space.

This is where A is on the piano.

☐ Playing exercise: Find A on your piano.

Video link: https://www.musicmousestudios.com/piano-instructional-videos

Music Notation Exercise

☐ Draw a treble clef followed by the notes C, D, E, F, G, and A

☐ Circle A.

Metronome

A metronome is a device that plays a constant beat and helps you play and practice music at a consistent tempo. **Tempo** refers to the speed at which you play a song. Sometimes when you're practicing, you may accidentally play at an uneven speed (for example, with a row of 8th notes, you may play the first and second ones fast but the last two slower because you're stumbling on the notes). Practicing with a metronome helps to ensure that you follow the beat and play every note in each respective rhythm evenly in speed.

There are various types of metronomes. Some are analog, and some are digital. Others you can download as an app on your phone. If you type "Metronome" in your App Store, you should be able to find metronome apps that are either free or very cheap. With each metronome, you can drag up or down the lever to raise or lower the number, which reflects the tempo or the BPM (beats per minute). A higher number indicates a faster tempo, while a lower number indicates a slower tempo.

If you happen to "fall off" the metronome train and either get behind or ahead of the beat, you can pause for a second and wait for the next beat to play the correct note in time. When practicing a new song, always put the metronome at a slow tempo (quarter note = 50 or lower is a good starting point) and practice at that speed until you can play every single note correctly. Only then should you gradually raise the tempo upon subsequent playthroughs of the music.

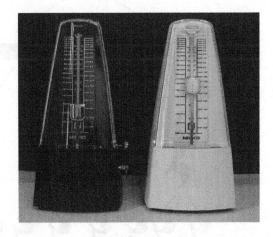

☐ Get a metronome – either buy one or download a metronome app on your phone (often, they are free).

☐ Set your metronome to 60 bpm. Follow the metronome's beat and clap through the full rhythm tree at this tempo.

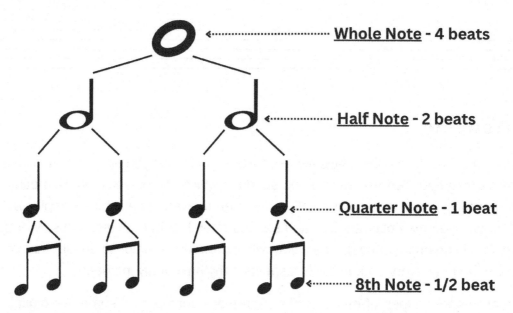

- **Whole Note** - 4 beats
- **Half Note** - 2 beats
- **Quarter Note** - 1 beat
- **8th Note** - 1/2 beat

☐ With your metronome still at 60 bpm, use your hands to silently "clap" through the full rests tree. Put both hands to the side every time you have to indicate a beat is passing.

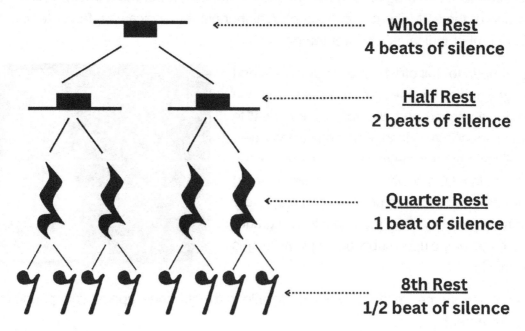

- **Whole Rest**
  4 beats of silence
- **Half Rest**
  2 beats of silence
- **Quarter Rest**
  1 beat of silence
- **8th Rest**
  1/2 beat of silence

Twinkle Twinkle Little Star

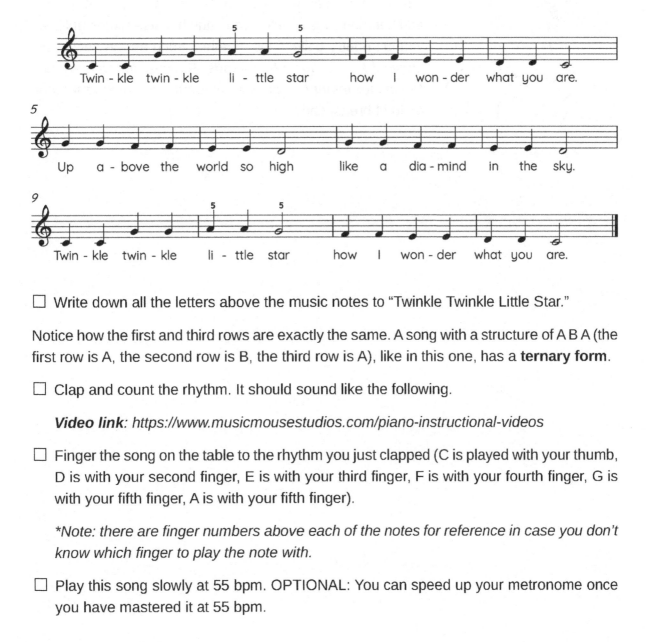

☐ Write down all the letters above the music notes to "Twinkle Twinkle Little Star."

Notice how the first and third rows are exactly the same. A song with a structure of A B A (the first row is A, the second row is B, the third row is A), like in this one, has a **ternary form**.

☐ Clap and count the rhythm. It should sound like the following.

Video link: https://www.musicmousestudios.com/piano-instructional-videos

☐ Finger the song on the table to the rhythm you just clapped (C is played with your thumb, D is with your second finger, E is with your third finger, F is with your fourth finger, G is with your fifth finger, A is with your fifth finger).

Note: there are finger numbers above each of the notes for reference in case you don't know which finger to play the note with.

☐ Play this song slowly at 55 bpm. OPTIONAL: You can speed up your metronome once you have mastered it at 55 bpm.

DAY 64

About Jane Taylor

Jane Taylor was a poet who lived from 1783 to 1824 in England. She is most widely known for having written the lyrics to "Twinkle Twinkle Little Star." She comes from a literary family – her sister was also a poet, her dad was an engraver, and her mom was a writer. Jane and her sister Ann published various poetry collections together, such as the successful *Original Poems for Infant Minds*, *Rhymes for Nursery* and *Hymns for Infant Minds*. She, unfortunately, died at the age of 40 of breast cancer.

New Song: "The Amazing Twinkle Twinkle Little Star"

We will now add some of the intervals we previously learned to "Twinkle Twinkle Little Star" to make it even more amazing!

☐ Look at the score below. Write down all the letters above the music notes. Notice how the first and the third rows are the same. Once again, we see that the song has a **ternary form**.

The Amazing Twinkle Twinkle Little Star

Arr. by Andrea Chang

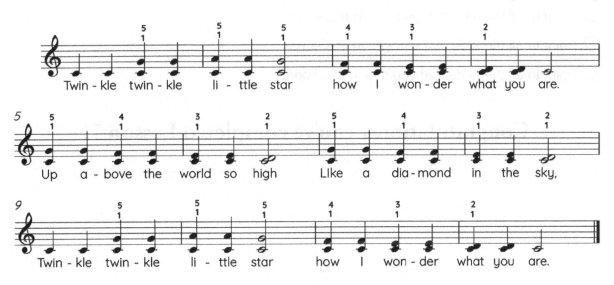

☐ Clap and count the rhythm. It should sound like the following.

Video link: https://www.musicmousestudios.com/piano-instructional-videos

☐ Finger the song on the table to the rhythm you just clapped (C is played with your thumb, D is with your second finger, E is with your third finger, F is with your fourth finger, G is with your fifth finger, A is with your fifth finger). Be sure to play all chords with the correct fingering.

Note: there are finger numbers above each of the notes for reference in case you don't know which finger to play the note with.

☐ Play this song slowly at 55 bpm. OPTIONAL: You can speed up your metronome once you have mastered it at 55 bpm.

In the second measure, when the notes are 6 letters apart from each other (for example, C to D to E to F to G to A), this interval is called a **6th**.

☐ Circle all the 6ths that you see in this song.

☐ Point to all the 5ths that you see in this song.

☐ Point to all the 4ths that you see in this song.

☐ Point to all the 3rds that you see in this song.

☐ Point to all the 2nds that you see in this song.

Congratulations, you've completed Lesson 7!

"When you have a dream, you've got to grab it and never let go."

—CAROL BURNETT

LESSON
8
The Memory Maze

But how do you remember what all of the notes are?! In this lesson,
we will go over tips and tricks on how to navigate this memory maze!

DAY 68

Introducing... the C Major Scale

What is a **scale**? The English alphabet has 26 letters. The musical alphabet has 7 letters, and these form a scale. In C Major, this scale consists of all the white notes on the piano – C, D, E, F, G, A, B. After B, it returns to C again, and the pattern continues until you run out of keys on the piano!

This week we will learn how to play an ascending C Major scale with our right hand!

To finger a C Major scale with your right hand, play the following notes with these fingers in this order:

Ascending

C – Finger 1

D – Finger 2

E – Finger 3

F – Finger 1 – you will cross your thumb underneath your third finger, which is on E, and place your thumb on F

G – Finger 2

A – Finger 3

B – Finger 4

C – Finger 5

This is what your finger should look like going from E to F with the thumb crossing under.

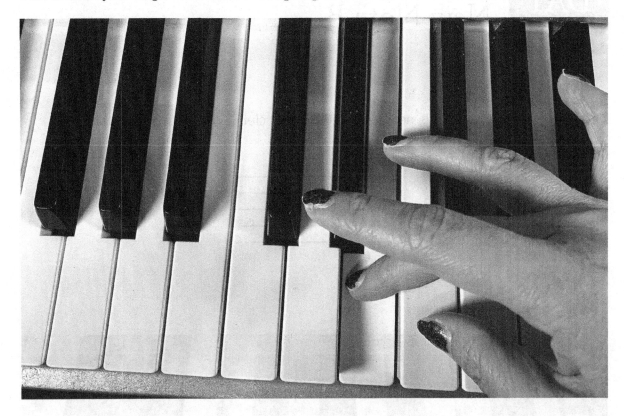

Today we are only focusing on ascending. We will practice descending in another lesson.

Watch this video to see it in action -

Video link: https://www.musicmousestudios.com/piano-instructional-videos

Warmup

☐ Play an ascending C Major Scale with your right hand 5 times, starting at middle C.

☐ With your left hand, play C D E F G (all these notes below middle C) ascending and then G F E D C descending all together 5 times. Practice slowly to ensure no sticky fingers!

C Major Scale Notation

This is what an ascending C Major Scale looks like written out on the treble clef staff.

C   D   E   F   G   A   B   C

DAY 69 New Note B

Our new note today is B! B is next to A. In the treble clef, it is written on the third line.

This is where B is on the piano.

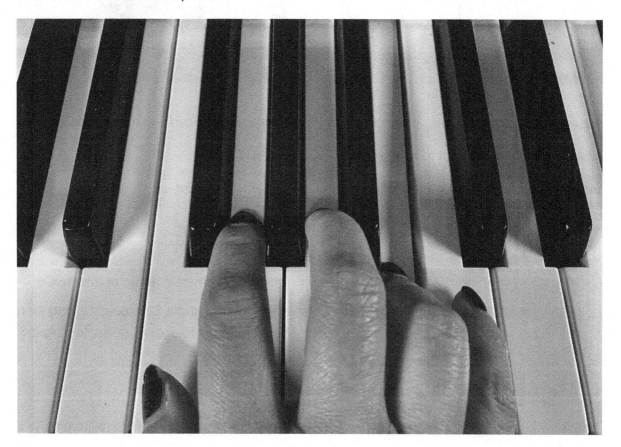

☐ Playing exercise: Find B on your piano and play it with your fourth finger in your right hand.

When the notes in the chord are 7 letters apart, this interval is called a **7th**. For example, C to B is a 7th because there are 7 letters from C (1) to D (2) to E (3) to F (4) to G (5) to A (6) to B (7).

☐ Playing exercise: Find middle C on the piano and then play the B you learned simultaneously. You will want to play C with your thumb and B with your pinky. It should look like the picture below.

Notes Above B

Now that you know the notes C, D, E, F, G, A, and B, the notes beyond B will keep repeating themselves with that pattern again, starting at C, up and down the piano for a C Major scale.

Regarding notation, if you continue to go up each space and line note, the written notes also keep repeating themselves. Every time the notes repeat themselves, we call this an **octave**. An octave is also an interval, similar to the 7th we just learned. An octave occurs when there are 8 steps in between the two notes. In our case, it is from middle C to the octave above middle C. Octaves, like the other intervals we've been learning, can be written harmonically (as a chord) or melodically (sequentially), as seen in the picture below.

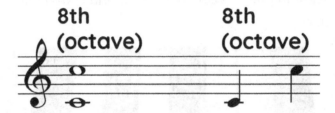

This is what it looks like on the piano – place your right thumb on middle C and your right pinky on the C above middle C. It is one key over to the right from playing a 7th.

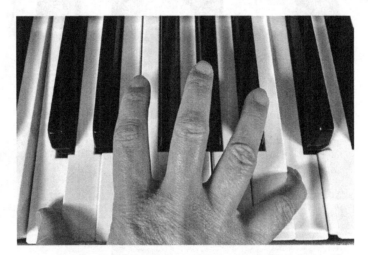

☐ Playing exercise #1: Play an octave with your right thumb on middle C and your right pinky on the C above middle C *at the same time.* This is a **harmonic octave.**

☐ Playing exercise #2: Now play middle C with your thumb, and then play the C above middle C with your pinky *after* that. This is a **melodic octave** because it is **arpeggiated**.

Extended Notes of the Scale

Look at the picture below to see what the notes of C Major (extended two octaves above middle C) on a treble clef look like on the staff.

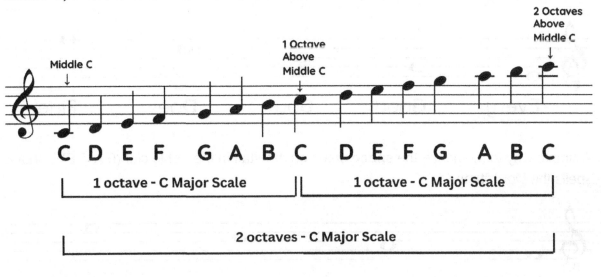

☐ Score exercise: Draw a treble clef and write 2 octaves of an ascending C Major scale below. Circle all the B's.

A full piano has 88 keys, consisting of 7 octaves and three lower notes below that (B, B flat, and A).

☐ Look at the graphic below and label all the notes on this 88 keys piano.

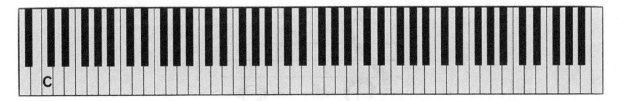

Now that you know what C, D, E, F, G, A, and B look like on the piano, it's time to memorize what they look like on the staff. Aside from remembering which space and line note goes with which letter notes, there are a couple of acronyms tricks that can help, which we will discuss in the next lesson!

DAY 72

Notes Acronyms:
Unlocking Memorization Tips

A simple way to memorize the **line** notes on the staff (E G B D F) in the treble clef is the following acronym "**E**very **G**ood **B**oy **D**oes **F**ine."

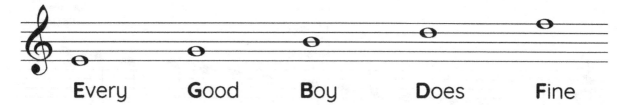

| Every | Good | Boy | Does | Fine |

A simple way to memorize the **space** notes on the staff in the treble clef (F A C E) is that it spells the word "**face**."

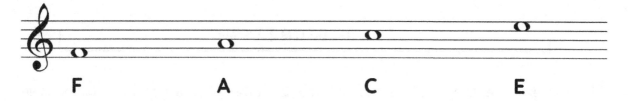

| F | A | C | E |

The "G Trick": Unlocking Memorization Tips

If all else fails and you still can't remember all of the notes, an easier way to figure out what the notes are in a treble clef is to remember that the treble clef is also known as the "G Clef." This is because where the treble clef curves inward is where the note G is located on the staff. Knowing where G is, you can count up or down on the staff to figure out the note in question.

Name that Note!

Let's practice! Feel free to use any of the above methods to determine the notes.

☐ Write down the letter name under each note below.

Answers

G D B F A E C C G E D F C A B

DAY 73-76

New Song: "Go Tell Aunt Rhody"

Take a look at this song, "Go Tell Aunt Rhody," below. Observe how it consists of three distinct sections – Part A, Part B, and a return to Part A again. It's helpful to distinguish the underlying structure of a song, as it identifies any recurring sections to save on practice time. Notice how it is broken apart into 3 sections – Part A, Part B, and then Part A again. Like "Twinkle, Twinkle Little Star," this song is in **ternary form**. On Day 73, practice Part A; on Day 74, practice Part B; on Day 75, practice Part A and putting it all together; on Day 76, solidify putting Part A, B, and A together and try to perform it for someone!

A note about fingering: fingering may change depending on what notes are in the song and how far you have to stretch your fingers in between notes. We may not always, for example, play C with our thumbs, D with our index fingers, E with our third fingers, etc. The fingering below is the smoothest route for your fingers to move quickly from one note to another for this particular song.

☐ Write down all the letters below the music notes for "Go Tell Aunt Rhody."

☐ Clap and count the rhythm. It should sound like the following.

   Video link: https://www.musicmousestudios.com/piano-instructional-videos

☐ Finger the song on the table to the rhythm you just clapped. *Follow the finger numbers listed above each of the notes.*

☐ Play this song slowly at 55 bpm. OPTIONAL: You can speed up your metronome once you have mastered it at 55 bpm.

Go Tell Aunt Rhody

Jean-Jacques Rousseau

About Jean-Jacques Rousseau

Jean-Jacques Rousseau, the composer of "Go Tell Aunt Rhody," lived from 1712 to 1778 and was born in Geneva. He was regarded as a philosopher, writer, and composer. His *Discourse on Inequality* and *The Social Contract* played an instrumental role in shaping the tenets of the Age of Enlightenment as well as parts of the French Revolution in regard to the economy, politics, and education.

Within *The Social Contract*, Rousseau proclaims, "Man is born free, and everywhere he is in chains. Those who think themselves the masters of others are indeed greater slaves than they." He believed that the establishment of various forms of government, be it monarchy, aristocracy, or democracy, stemmed from inequalities in society, which would inevitably spark new revolutions aimed at toppling existing systems, only to find that the new leaders would perpetuate and exacerbate the very disparities they sought to rectify. Nevertheless, Rousseau was convinced that humanity possessed an innate desire for progress, which would create improved political systems that genuinely served the collective welfare.

As a composer, Rousseau's music was a fusion of Baroque and Classical styles. Much like his philosophical pursuits, the concept of freedom is a pillar in many of his musical works. There is an emphasis on the melody, which laid the foundation for the Romantic period, where expression eclipsed the rigid constraints and methodologies of the Baroque and Classical eras. Rousseau composed seven operas, drawing recognition from luminaries such as Mozart and Beethoven. Beethoven himself crafted a standalone song from Rousseau's one-act opera "The Village Soothsayer" and titled it "Non, Colette n'est point trompeuse." It is within this same opera that the melody for "Go Tell Aunt Rhody" comes from.

Congratulations, you've completed Lesson 8!

"Believe you can and you're halfway there."

—THEODORE ROOSEVELT

LESSON
9
Dual Hand Artistry

The spotlight now shines on the left hand! This lesson is dedicated to all the left-handed players as we explore the art of incorporating the left alongside the right hand for a harmonious union of musical expression.

Descending C Major Scale Right Hand

But first, let's finish out our C Major scale with our right hand. A descending C Major Scale with your right hand is the same as ascending except in reverse order. See below for the fingering.

Descending

C (above middle C) – Finger 5

B (above middle C) – Finger 4

A (above middle C) – Finger 3

G (above middle C) – Finger 2

F (above middle C) – Finger 1

E (above middle C) – Finger 3 – your 3rd finger will cross over your thumb

D (above middle C) – Finger 2

C (middle C) – Finger 1

In the figure below, the fingering will start on the right side and go toward the left.

The main place to pay attention to is going from F back down to E and crossing that **3rd** finger over your thumb, as seen in the picture below.

Video link: *https://www.musicmousestudios.com/piano-instructional-videos*

Warmup – Review

☐ Practice playing a descending C Major scale with your right hand 5 times, starting at the C above middle C.

☐ Play an ascending and descending C Major scale with your right hand 5 times.

☐ With your left hand, play C D E F G (all these notes below middle C) ascending and then descending G F E D C 5 times. Practice slowly to ensure no sticky fingers!

DAY 79

New Note C in Bass Clef

Middle C is the same note we played on the piano with our right hand, but this time we will play it with our left hand.

☐ Playing exercise #1: Find middle C and then play it with your left thumb.

☐ Playing exercise #2: Now find the C below that. Play this lower C with your pinky. This is the same C you've been playing in your warm-ups with your left hand.

This is what the notes look like on the staff. Notice how these two C's make an **octave**. Similar to our lesson with right hand octaves, the left hand can also be written as broken or arpeggiated melodic octaves or stacked together like a chord for harmonic octaves.

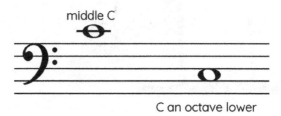

Playing Octaves

You can play octaves on any note, with any hand. Generally, when playing octaves, you will play with your thumb and pinky so that your hand can stretch across all the notes more easily. In your left hand, the pinky is on the bottom note of the octave, and the thumb is on the top note of the octave. In your right hand, it's the opposite, with your thumb on the bottom note of the octave and your pinky on the top note of the octave.

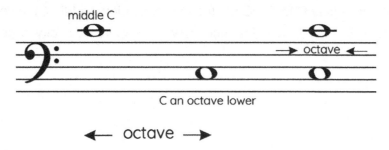

Now that we know how to play octaves with both hands, let's discuss the octave symbol. When the composer wants you to play a series of notes an octave higher, they will sometimes use an octave *above* symbol with a line above all the notes that should be played an octave higher. The "a" in "8va" is used to represent an octave "above."

With the *8va* symbol, the notes below are what it should actually sound like

Conversely, when the composer wants you to play a series of notes an octave *lower*, they will use an octave *below* symbol with a line below all the notes that should be played an octave lower. The "b" in "8vb" is used to represent an octave "below."

With the *8vb* symbol, it should sound like the notes below. We haven't covered the bass clef notes yet, but they are basically the C Major scale notes sounding an octave lower, as seen below.

☐ Play a C Major scale an octave above middle C (as written below).

☐ Play a C Major scale an octave below middle C (as written below).

Video link: *https://www.musicmousestudios.com/piano-instructional-videos*

New Note B in Bass Clef

In the last lesson, we learned where B is in the Treble Clef. Today, we will be playing B in the Bass Clef.

☐ Playing exercise #1: Find middle C and then play it with your thumb.

☐ Playing exercise #2: Play the note next to middle C with your second finger. This is B. Refer to the picture below.

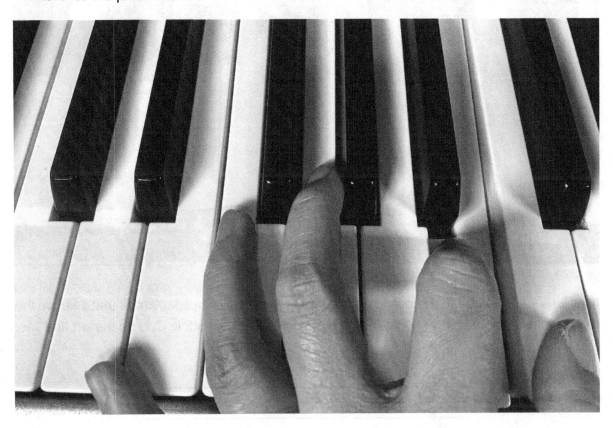

☐ Playing exercise #3: Now we will play the B an octave below the B you just played. Because we're playing an octave, we will use our thumb and pinky. Instead of using your second finger on B, shift your thumb over to that B. Now with your pinky, stretch it down to the B an octave below.

Video link: *https://www.musicmousestudios.com/piano-instructional-videos*

Now let's see what these B's look like on the Bass Clef staff. The space note that's above the top line is the B right below middle C. The B, an octave below middle C, is on the second line.

B right below middle C

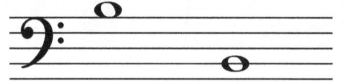

B an octave lower

Played together as a stacked B octave chord, it looks like the following:

Music Notation Exercise

Since we are playing with our left hand, we need to draw a bass clef. As seen above, a bass clef looks like an F with 2 dots on the top 2 spaces of the staff.

☐ Draw a bass clef.

☐ Draw a middle C whole note.

☐ Draw a whole note on the C below middle C and stack it as an octave chord below the middle C you drew.

☐ Draw a whole note B (the B right below middle C).

☐ Draw a whole note B, an octave below the B you just drew, and stack it as an octave chord.

Rhythm Exercises

For each of the rhythm exercises below:

☐ Clap and count them aloud.

☐ Play them slowly on the piano.

Video link: *https://www.musicmousestudios.com/piano-instructional-videos*

Notice how the notes are all in octaves, either on C or B, with the octaves to be played with your pinky and thumb.

The Grand Staff

When we put the Treble Clef and Bass Clef staffs together and combine them with a **brace**, we form what's called the **Grand Staff**. The Grand Staff indicates that we play with both our right and left hands.

brace -> Grand Staff

New Song: "Ode to Joy" (Both Hands)

You played this song in a previous lesson, but now we will add the left hand and play it together with the right hand!

☐ Write down all the letters below the music notes.

☐ Clap and count the rhythm of the right hand.

☐ Clap and count the rhythm of the left hand.

☐ Finger the right hand on the table (C with your thumb, D with your 2nd finger, E with your 3rd finger, F with your 4th finger, and G with your pinky).

☐ Finger the left hand on the table (All C and B octaves should be played with your pinky and thumb).

☐ Play this song slowly with your left hand first. You can move on to the right hand once you feel comfortable with your left.

☐ Play this song slowly with your right hand.

☐ Play this song slowly with hands together. OPTIONAL: You can speed it up once you have mastered it.

Video link: https://www.musicmousestudios.com/piano-instructional-videos

Ode to Joy

Ludwig van Beethoven
arr. by Andrea Chang

Congratulations, you've completed Lesson 9!

"Nothing is impossible.
The word itself says: 'I'm possible!'"

—AUDREY HEPBURN

LESSON
10
The Ambidextrous Mastery

The marvels of our brain never cease to amaze, enabling us to send neuro signals throughout our entire body, orchestrating the actions of various body parts. In the upcoming lesson, let's enhance our coordination skills and direct our attention toward achieving harmony between our left and right hands on the piano!

☐ Play a C Major Scale (ascending and descending) with your right hand 5 times, starting at middle C.

☐ With your left hand, play C D E F G ascending and descending G F E D C 5 times. Practice slowly to ensure no sticky fingers!

In our warmups, we played C D E F G in our left hand. We will learn about that same G today. Like C and B from the last lesson, we can also play G an octave lower.

☐ Playing exercise #1: Find middle C and then play it with your thumb.

☐ Playing exercise #2: Keep your thumb on middle C and play down to your fourth finger. This is the G below middle C. Refer to the picture below.

☐ Playing exercise #3: Shift your 4th finger to your left **thumb** on the G below middle C, and stretch your pinky down to the G an octave below.

This is what the notes look like on the staff. Notice how these two G's make an **octave**. Like with other notes, they can be written arpeggiated as a melodic octave or stacked together like a chord as a harmonic octave.

G right below middle C   G octave

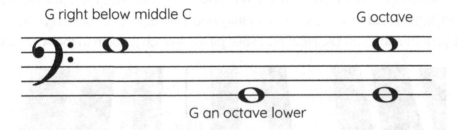

G an octave lower

Video link: https://www.musicmousestudios.com/piano-instructional-videos

DAY 88

New Note A in Bass Clef

Previously, we learned how to play B in the bass clef. If we go one note down from B, we are at A.

☐ Playing exercise #1: Find middle C and then play it with your thumb.

☐ Playing exercise #2: Keep your thumb on middle C and play down to your third finger. This is the A below middle C. Refer to the picture below.

☐ Playing exercise #3: Now let's play the A an octave below the A you just played. Because we're playing an octave, we will use our pinky and thumb. Instead of using your 3rd finger on A, shift your thumb to that A. Now with your pinky, stretch it down to the A an octave below.

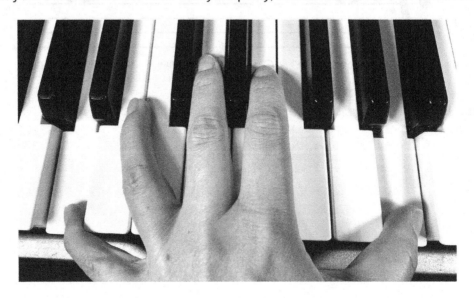

This is what the A's should look like on the staff.

A below middle C   A an octave below middle C   A octave

Video link: *https://www.musicmousestudios.com/piano-instructional-videos*

Music Notation Exercise

☐ Draw a bass clef.

☐ Draw a whole note for the A below middle C.

☐ Draw a whole note for the A, an octave below that, and stack it below as an octave chord.

☐ Draw a whole note G below middle C.

☐ Draw the G an octave below that and stack it as an octave chord.

DAY 89-90 Rhythm Exercises

For each of the rhythm exercises below:

☐ Clap and count them aloud.

☐ Play them slowly on the piano.

Video link: https://www.musicmousestudios.com/piano-instructional-videos

Note: The first two exercises have octave chords on A or G.

The second two exercises have octave notes arpeggiated on A, G, C, or B.

All octaves should be played with your pinky and thumb.

When we have a repeated pattern of notes, like in Exercises 3 and 4, we call that an **ostinato.** Sometimes in piano, you will find ostinatos that occur in your left hand, which we will see in the next song we will be learning.

New Song: "Go Tell Aunt Rhody" (Both Hands)

We will continue playing "Go Tell Aunt Rhody" this week and add in the left hand! On Day 91, practice Part A; on Day 92, practice Part B; on Day 93, practice Part A and putting it together; on Day 94, solidify putting Part A, B, and A together and try to perform it for someone!

Video link: https://www.musicmousestudios.com/piano-instructional-videos

☐ Write down all the letters below the music notes.

☐ Clap and count the rhythm of the right hand.

☐ Clap and count the rhythm of the left hand.

☐ Fill out the rest of the fingering in the song. The right hand fingering is provided. The left hand fingering consists of octaves played as chords and arpeggios with the thumb and 5th finger.

☐ Finger the right hand on the table.

☐ Finger the left hand on the table.

☐ Finger both hands together on the table.

☐ Play this song slowly with your left hand first. You can move on to the right once you feel comfortable with your left hand.

☐ Play this song slowly with your right hand.

☐ Play this song slowly with both hands together. OPTIONAL: You can speed it up once you have mastered it.

Go Tell Aunt Rhody

for Piano

Jean-Jacques Rousseau
Arranged by Andrea Chang

Part A

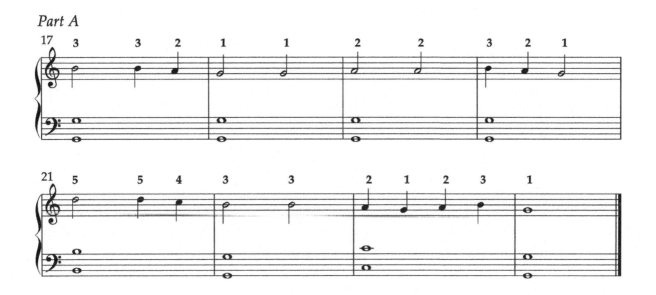

Congratulations, you've completed Lesson 10!

"I can accept failure;
everyone fails at something.
But I can't accept not trying."

—MICHAEL JORDAN

LESSON
11
The Power of 3

Get ready to immerse yourself in the captivating realm of threes! In this upcoming lesson, we will delve into a fresh time signature and discover ties and a new rhythm that will broaden your rhythmic horizons!

C Major Scale Left Hand

To finger a C Major scale with your left hand, play the following notes with these fingers in this order:

Ascending

C (below middle C) – Finger 5

D (below middle C) – Finger 4

E (below middle C) – Finger 3

F (below middle C) – Finger 2

G (below middle C) – Finger 1

A (below middle C) – Finger 3 (cross over Finger 1)

B (below middle C) – Finger 2

C (middle C) – Finger 1

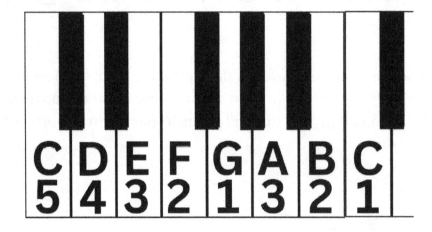

This is what your finger should look like going from G to A with the 3rd finger crossing over the thumb.

Today, we are only focusing on ascending. We will practice descending in another lesson.

Warmup Review

☐ Play a C Major Scale with your right hand (ascending and descending) 5 times.

☐ Play an ascending C Major Scale with your left hand 5 times. Practice slowly to ensure no sticky fingers!

Video link: *https://www.musicmousestudios.com/piano-instructional-videos*

DAY 96 Intervals Review

☐ Label these ascending intervals.

☐ Check your answers.

5th   3rd   4th   2nd   7th   octave   6th   3rd

☐ Label these descending intervals.

☐ Check your answers.

2nd   4th   octave   7th   5th   3rd   3rd   6th

☐ Label these interval chords.

— — — — — —

☐ Check your answers.

octave 6th 2nd 7th 3rd 4th 5th

☐ Fill in the missing **top** note to create these interval chords.

5th 3rd 4th 2nd 7th octave 6th

☐ Check your answers.

5th 3rd 4th 2nd 7th octave 6th

☐ Fill in the missing **bottom** note to create these interval chords.

example: 3rd 2nd 4th 7th 5th 6th
octave

☐ Check your answers.

example: 3rd 2nd 4th 7th 5th 6th
octave

DAY 97

Dotted Half Note

Today, we're learning a new rhythm called a dotted half note! Its name is derived from the fact that it consists of a half note followed by a dot. A dotted half note is held for 3 beats.

$\frac{3}{4}$ Time Signature

All the music we've been playing thus far has been in the time signature 4/4. Today, we will explore a new time signature, 3/4. As previously mentioned, in a time signature, the top number tells us how many beats are in a measure, and the bottom number tells us the unit of time or which note receives one beat. In 3/4, the 3 on top tells us that there are 3 beats per measure, and the 4 on the bottom signifies that the quarter note gets the beat.

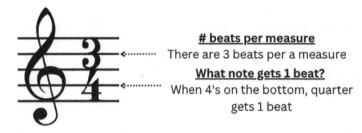

 # beats per measure
There are 3 beats per a measure
What note gets 1 beat?
When 4's on the bottom, quarter gets 1 beat

3/4 feels a lot different than 4/4. Songs written in 3/4 often include waltzes, where you really feel that first beat in the 3-beat pattern.

Dotted half notes frequently occur in 3/4. We will look at a song today that uses both 3/4 and dotted half notes.

Play These Dotted Half Notes!

☐ Label all the letters underneath the notes.

☐ Play the exercise below using the fingering provided.

Video link: https://www.musicmousestudios.com/piano-instructional-videos

When you want notes to sustain for longer than their expected duration, you can add a **tie** and connect it to the following note. For example, if I had a dotted half note and I wanted that note to be 2 beats longer, I would tie a half note next to that dotted half note. This tie signifies that you will hold the duration of the first note (dotted half note) in addition to the duration of the second note (half note). Let's clap and count some examples below:

1   In this first example, you will hold the note for 6 beats total (3 beats for the first measure tied to 3 beats in the second measure). Try clapping and counting this (you will only clap once and hold that clap for 6 beats).

Video link: *https://www.musicmousestudios.com/piano-instructional-videos*

2   Notice how ties can face upward (like in the previous example) or downward (like in the example below). They will generally follow the opposite direction of the stems of the notes they tie together. In this second example, you will hold the note for 5 beats total (3 beats for the first measure and 2 beats for the second measure). Try clapping and counting this!

3   In this third example, you will hold the note for 4 beats total (3 beats for the first measure and 1 beat for the second measure). Try clapping and counting this!

4 In this fourth example, you will hold the note for 3.5 beats total (3 beats for the first measure and 1/2 beat for the second measure). Try clapping and counting this!

How Many Beats?

Fill in the blanks with the total number of beats you should hold each tie for.

1

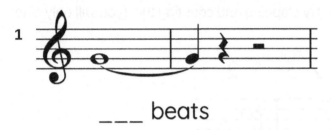

_____ beats

2

_____ beats

3

_____ beats

4

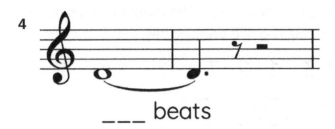

_____ beats

5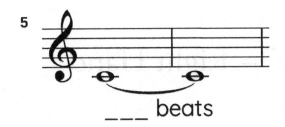

_ _ _ beats

6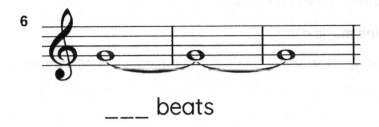

_ _ _ beats

Answers

1 5 beats

2 7 beats

3 6 beats

4 5.5 beats

5 8 beats

6 12 beats

DAY 99-101

New Song:
"Amazing Grace" – Right Hand

Today, we will learn just the right hand to "Amazing Grace."

☐ Write down all the letters below the music notes.

☐ Circle the time signature of the song. How many beats are in a measure? Which note gets the beat?

☐ Circle any ties you see in the song.

☐ Clap and count the rhythm. It should sound like the following.

Video link: https://www.musicmousestudios.com/piano-instructional-videos

☐ Finger the music on the table to the rhythm you just clapped. Follow the fingering provided.

Amazing Grace
for Piano

John Newton
Arranged by Andrea Chang

☐ Play this song slowly. OPTIONAL: You can speed it up once you have mastered it.

John Newton, the author behind the timeless hymn "Amazing Grace," was born in London in 1725. He grew up at sea, sailing alongside his father, starting at the age of 11. His mother brought him up in Christianity as a child, but her untimely death when Newton was at the tender age of seven caused him to largely forsake his faith. Newton began working on slave ships and eventually became Captain of several of them. Sailing around Africa, he sought out and captured slaves and sold them to make a profit.

One fateful day, he encountered a ferocious storm. Some of his crew went overboard, and their ship was on the brink of sinking. As Newton frantically tried to steer the ship, he shouted, "Lord, have mercy on us!" After 11 hours of continuing to struggle, Newton finally got the

crew back to safety. This transformative experience prompted Newton to turn his life around and become a Christian. Newton set March 21st, the day of this life-altering event, as a day he would remember to pray and praise God. Newton also later exited the slave trade industry and fervently advocated for the abolition of slavery. He then learned Hebrew and Greek and became ordained as a pastor, leading his own church.

In 1767, a poet named William Cowper, who frequented Newton's church, collaborated with Newton to create a remarkable collection of hymns, which came to be known as the *Olney Hymns*. This volume was published in 1779, and nestled within its pages lay the verses of "Amazing Grace," initially titled "Faith's Review and Expectation."

Congratulations, you've completed Lesson 11!

"Tough times never last, but tough people do."

—ROBERT H. SCHULLER

LESSON
12
Harmonic Horizons

In our upcoming lesson, we will dig deeply into the realm of
chords to expand your understanding of harmonics!

DAY 103   C Major Scale Left Hand

To finger a descending C Major scale with your left hand, play the following notes with these fingers in this order:

Descending

C (middle C) – Finger 1

B (below middle C) – Finger 2

A (below middle C) – Finger 3

G (below middle C) – Finger 1

F (below middle C) – Finger 2

E (below middle C) – Finger 3

D (below middle C) – Finger 4

C (below middle C) – Finger 5

This is what your finger should look like going from A to G with the thumb crossing under the 3rd finger.

Warmup Review

For the following, practice slowly to ensure no sticky fingers!

☐ Play a descending C Major Scale with your left hand 5 times.

☐ Play an ascending C Major Scale followed by a descending C Major Scale with your left hand 5 times.

☐ Play a C Major Scale with your right hand, ascending and descending 5 times.

☐ Play a C Major scale ascending and descending with both hands.

Video link: *https://www.musicmousestudios.com/piano-instructional-videos*

New Note D in Bass Clef

Today, we will learn where D is on the piano and on the staff.

☐ Playing exercise #1: Find the D above middle C and play it with your thumb.

☐ Playing exercise #2: Stretch your pinky an octave below that D and play it simultaneously with the higher D. Refer to the picture below.

Video link: https://www.musicmousestudios.com/piano-instructional-videos

This is what the notes look like on the staff.

D above middle C   D an octave below middle C   D octave

Music Notation Exercise

☐ On the staff below, draw a bass clef.

☐ Draw the D above middle C.

☐ Draw the D an octave below that D and stack it as an octave chord.

Chord Structures

In a scale, certain notes are essential for making a chord. These notes are 1, 3, and 5. A three-note chord is called a **triad**.

Let's take the C Major scale that we have been playing. **Note:** This is NOT fingering numbers. This is simply the notes labeled by the order they come on the scale. For example, C will be 1 because it's the first note in the C Major scale. D will be 2 because it's the second note in the scale, and so and so forth.

C – 1

D – 2

E – 3

F – 4

G – 5

A – 6

B – 7

☐ Circle the 1, 3, and 5 notes above.

The 1, 3, and 5 notes in a C Major scale are C, E, and G. We can use these to build a triad. We can also rearrange the 1, 3, and 5 notes in different orders to create variations of C Major chords. Each of these variations has a name.

When 1 is on the bottom of the triad, we say this chord is in **root** position. When 3 is on the bottom, the chord is in **first inversion**. When 5 is on the bottom, the chord is in **second inversion**. We can apply this to chords both in the treble and the bass clef.

Sometimes, notes from the triad (out of 1, 3, 5) can be missing. However, we can still deduce that the chord is in C Major since it is implied by the presence of the other notes in the triad, as seen in the last three chords of the row. Notice also how in the second inversion chord in the bass clef, the top note is an E, a note we haven't covered yet, but if you count up from middle C, it is on the ledger line right above it. Refer to the picture below for all the different chord inversions of C Major.

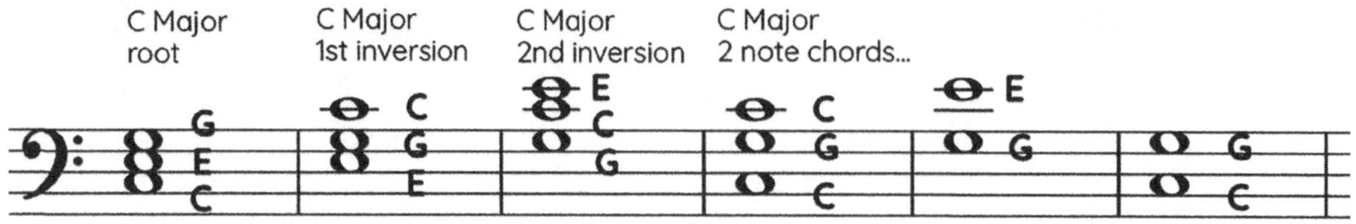

LESSON 12

Chord Playing Exercises

Review the C Major chords from the last lesson and familiarize yourself with the notes. Let's try playing some of these chords below. If you'd like, write the letter notes in the exercises below to reinforce them. Follow the fingering provided.

Video link: https://www.musicmousestudios.com/piano-instructional-videos

Chord Playing Exercises

We can also apply this to other starting notes. For example, if G is our root note, then we are in the key of G Major. We would label all of the letters of the scale in G Major as the following:

G – 1

A – 2

B – 3

C – 4

D – 5

E – 6

F♯ (we will cover what ♯ is in the next lesson) – 7

The 1, 3, and 5 notes are G, B, and D. Knowing this, we can also play through the various inversions of a G Major chord (root, 1st, 2nd, and those with missing notes), as seen in the picture below.

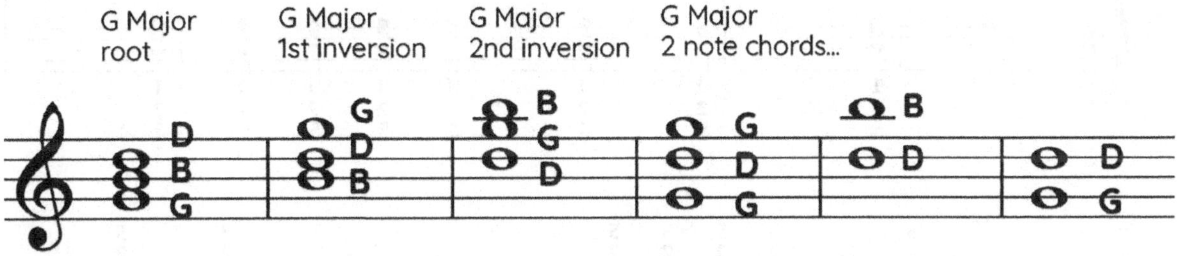

Refer to the G Major chords above and familiarize yourself with the notes. Let's try playing some of these exercises. If you'd like, write down the letter notes in the exercises below to further reinforce them. Follow the fingering provided.

Video link: https://www.musicmousestudios.com/piano-instructional-videos

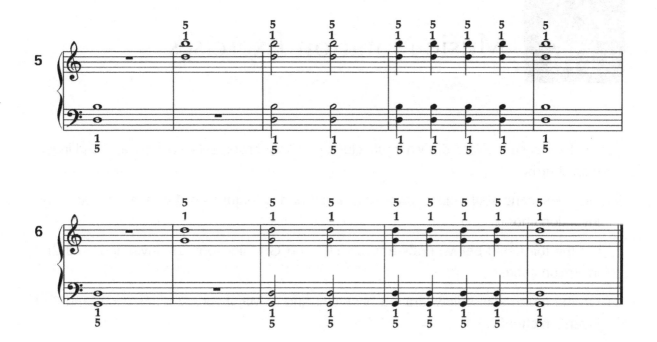

DAY 110 Music Notation Exercises

☐ On the first staff below, draw a treble clef and C Major root, 1st inversion, and 2nd inversion chords.

☐ On the second staff below, draw a bass clef and C Major root, 1st inversion, and 2nd inversion chords.

☐ On the third staff below, draw a treble clef and G Major root, 1st inversion, and 2nd inversion chords.

☐ On the fourth staff below, draw a bass clef and G Major root, 1st inversion, and 2nd inversion chords.

New Song:
"Amazing Grace" – Left Hand

DAY
111-113

Today we will put the left and right hand together to "Amazing Grace!" Notice how in the left hand, even though there are 3 notes, they consist of 2 letter notes, creating the "implied" G Major chords we discussed earlier.

☐ Write down all the letters above or below the music notes.

☐ Circle the time signature of the song. How many beats are in a measure? Which note gets the beat?

☐ Circle any ties you see in the song.

Video link: https://www.musicmousestudios.com/piano-instructional-videos

☐ Clap and count the rhythm of the right hand.

☐ Clap and count the rhythm of the left hand.

☐ Clap and count the rhythm of both hands on the table.

☐ Finger the right hand on the table. Follow the fingering provided.

☐ Finger the left hand on the table. You will be using the same fingering for each chord in the song, so from the bottom to top, the fingers 5, 2, and 1, respectively, will be used to play each chord in the song.

☐ Finger the song with both hands on the table.

☐ Play this song slowly with your left hand first.

☐ Play this song slowly with your right hand.

☐ Play this song slowly with hands together. OPTIONAL: You can speed it up once you have mastered it.

Amazing Grace

for Piano

John Newton
Arranged by Andrea Chang

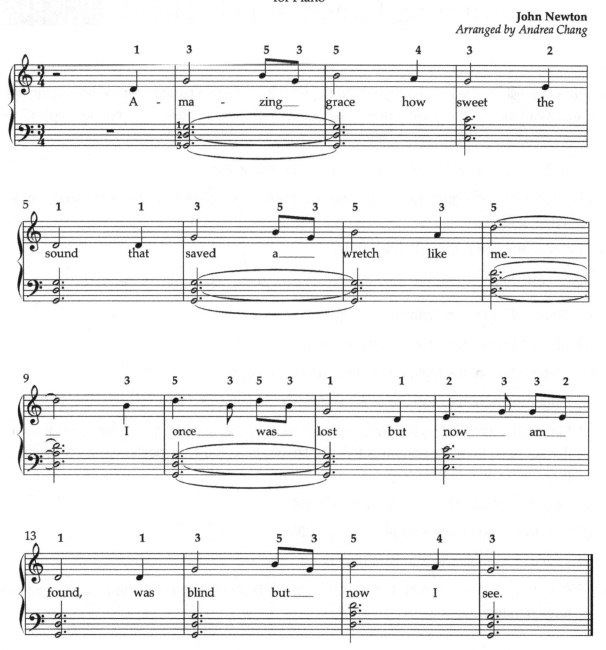

Repeat Sign Symbols

If you are familiar with the song "Amazing Grace," you may have noticed that it contains multiple verses, as seen in the music below (on Day 115). **Repeat signs** are placed at the beginning and end of the sections the composer wishes to repeat to save space and avoid duplicating the same music for each verse. In the case of "Amazing Grace," the entire song is repeated because there are repeat symbols at the beginning and the end of the piece. This practice is commonly found in hymns, where the lyrics for each verse are listed in between the staffs, and a repeat sign is used to indicate that the same music should be played for each verse. A repeat sign consists of two dots placed in the middle two spaces of the staff. The beginning repeat sign appears before two bar lines, while the ending repeat sign is followed by two bar lines.

1st and 2nd Endings

Additionally, in the music below, you may have noticed other markings at the end of the piece, specifically brackets with numbers inside, positioned above the last two measures. The first bracket contains the numbers 1, 2, and 3 and indicate different endings for the piece, known as 1st and 2nd Endings, depending on how many times the music has been repeated. In our case, during the first three repetitions of the piece, you will play the same ending, as indicated in measure 16 (the measure with the bracket displaying 1, 2, 3 above it). On the fourth repetition of the piece, you will skip measure 16 and play measure 17 instead (the final measure with the bracket and the number 4 on top of it).

New Song: "Amazing Grace"
(Multiple Verses)

Amazing Grace
for Piano

John Newton
Arranged by Andrea Chang

☐ Circle where the repeat signs are.

☐ Play Amazing Grace through all its verses using the repeat signs and 1st, 2nd, 3rd, and 4th endings.

☐ Perform this for someone or share this with us on our website!

Video link: *https://www.musicmousestudios.com/piano-instructional-videos*

DAY 117 Warmup Review

☐ Play a C Major Scale with both hands ascending and descending 5 times.

New Note E in Bass Clef

Today, we will learn the last two notes in the bass clef – E and F.

☐ Playing exercise #1: Find the E above middle C and play it with your left thumb.

☐ Playing exercise #2: Stretch your pinky an octave below that E and play it simultaneously as the higher E. Refer to the picture below.

Below is what E looks like written out on the staff. The first chord on the left is what we just played on the piano. Because this chord is a bit higher (notice the ledger line E on top, you may prefer to play it an octave lower, which is the chord displayed in the staff on the right.

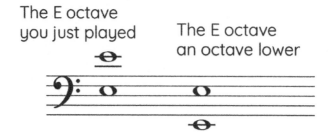

Video link: *https://www.musicmousestudios.com/piano-instructional-videos*

New Note F in Bass Clef

Now, for the final white note in our left hand... we will learn F!

☐ Playing exercise #1: Find the F above middle C and play it with your left thumb.

☐ Playing exercise #2: Stretch your pinky an octave below that F and play it at the same time as the higher F. Refer to the picture below.

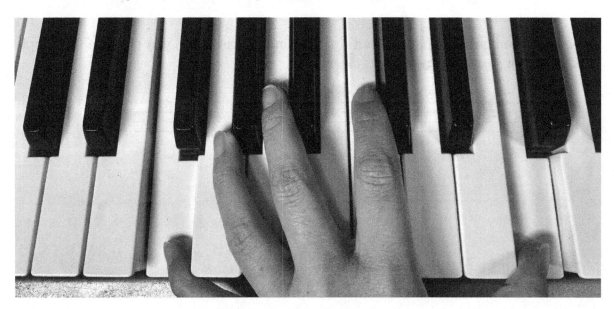

Below is what F looks like on the staff. The first chord on the left is what we just played on the piano. Because this chord is a bit higher (notice the ledger line F on top, you may prefer to play it an octave lower, which is the chord displayed in the staff on the right.

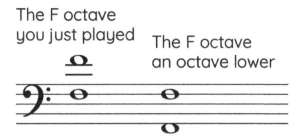

The F octave you just played

The F octave an octave lower

Video link: *https://www.musicmousestudios.com/piano-instructional-videos*

Notes Acronyms: Memorization Tips for Bass Clef Notes

Now that we've covered all of the white notes in the bass clef, you can use any of the acronyms below to remember the **line notes** GBDFA in the Bass Clef. Choose your favorite!

Good	**B**oys	**D**o	**F**ine	**A**lways
Good	**B**ikes	**D**on't	**F**all	**A**part
Grizzly	**B**ears	**D**on't	**F**ly	**A**irplanes

To easily remember the **space notes** A C E G in the Bass Clef, you can use the simple mnemonic "All Cows Eat Grass."

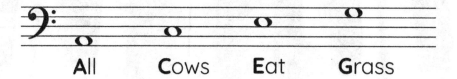

| **A**ll | **C**ows | **E**at | **G**rass |

Performance (OPTIONAL)

Practice all of the songs and perform them for someone or share it with us on our website, www.musicmousestudios.com!

- ☐ Mary Had a Little Lamb
- ☐ Down the River
- ☐ Oh When the Saints Go Marching In
- ☐ Twinkle, Twinkle Little Star

- ☐ The Amazing Twinkle, Twinkle Little Star
- ☐ Ode to Joy
- ☐ Go Tell Aunt Rhody
- ☐ Amazing Grace

Congratulations, you've completed Lesson 12!

"It always seems impossible until it's done."

—NELSON MANDELA

CERTIFICATE
OF AWARD

presented to :

Congratulations! You have graduated from Book 1 -
Your Golden Ears: First Piano Lessons for Adult Beginners!

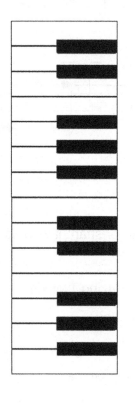

Andrea Chang

Founder of
Music Mouse Studios

Date

Leave A 1-Click Review!

I would be incredibly thankful if you could just take 60 seconds to write a brief review on Amazon, even if it's just a few sentences.

Customer reviews

★★★★★ 5 out of 5

2 global ratings

5 star	████████████	100%
4 star		0%
3 star		0%
2 star		0%
1 star		0%

˅ How customer reviews and ratings work

Review this product

Share your thoughts with other customers

Conclusion – Beyond the Last Note

Congratulations, you did it!!! That was not an easy feat completing this course, but you persevered and nailed it!! We have covered a wide range of essential topics, including selecting the right piano or keyboard for your needs and exploring various options available. You have learned how to confidently navigate the piano, playing and reading notes in both your left and right hands. The basics of music theory have been demystified, enabling you to understand the structure and elements of music.

We have also focused on honing your technical skills and finger dexterity through our carefully crafted warmups and playing exercises. By practicing these exercises, you have developed the foundation necessary for playing more complex pieces with confidence and precision. Additionally, we have delved into the realm of music analysis and music theory, empowering you to appreciate and interpret compositions with a deeper understanding.

Furthermore, this book has allowed you to explore the enchanting world of classical music. You have been introduced to timeless masterpieces and had the opportunity to learn about the fascinating backgrounds of renowned composers. By connecting with their stories, you have gained a greater appreciation for the rich history and emotions encapsulated within each musical work.

As you conclude this book, remember that your journey as a pianist is just beginning! It is crucial to continue learning, practicing, and pushing your boundaries. Don't be discouraged by challenges; instead, see them as stepping stones to growth and improvement. You now possess the tools and knowledge to apply what you have learned, and this book will serve as a valuable resource you can always refer back to.

Put into practice all that you have learned and persistently pursue excellence in your piano playing. Embrace the opportunity to apply your knowledge, honing your skills with dedication and a commitment to continuous improvement. Your journey toward mastery awaits, and we believe in your ability to achieve greatness in your musical endeavors! Share your progress with us, inspire others, and continue to pursue your musical dreams with passion and determination!!

If you have found value in this book, we kindly ask for your support. Please consider leaving a positive review on Amazon and subscribing to our YouTube channel, where you will find more valuable content and piano lessons! Visit us at https://www.youtube.com/@ homeschoolingwithandrea.

For personalized assistance, additional resources, and support, we invite you to explore our website, *www.musicmousestudios.com*. You will find a wealth of information to aid you on your musical journey.

And don't forget about your free gift!

To receive this exclusive download of additional sheet music and songs, simply visit *https://www.musicmousestudios.com/contact* and include the text "SHEET MUSIC" in your message.

We have thoroughly enjoyed being a part of your piano journey so far, and we are excited to continue supporting you as you grow and excel as a pianist. The best is yet to come!

Keep playing, keep learning,
and keep reaching for the stars!

References

Sarah Josepha Hale: The Godmother of Thanksgiving. (n.d.). Almanac.com. https://www.almanac. com/sarah-josepha-hale-godmother-thanksgiving#:~:text=In%201863%2C%20with%20 the%20country,Lincoln%20liked%20Hale's%20idea.

Wikipedia contributors. (2023). Sarah Josepha Hale. *Wikipedia.* https://en.wikipedia.org/wiki/ Sarah_Josepha_Hale

Amelinckx, A. (2018, October 2). *The True Story Behind "Mary Had a Little Lamb" – Modern Farmer.* Modern Farmer. https://modernfarmer.com/2017/12/ true-story-behind-mary-little-lamb/

Wikipedia contributors. (2023b). Ludwig van Beethoven. *Wikipedia.* https://en.m.wikipedia.org/ wiki/Ludwig_van_Beethoven

Ludwig van Beethoven | Biography, Music, & Facts. (2023, April 25). Encyclopedia Britannica. https://www.britannica.com/biography/Ludwig-van-Beethoven/Early-influences

The remarkable story of Beethoven's 'Choral' Symphony No. 9 and the 'Ode to Joy.' (n.d.). Classic FM. https://www.classicfm.com/composers/beethoven/music/symphony-no-9-d-minor/

Wikipedia contributors. (2023c). Helene von Breuning. *Wikipedia.* https://en.m.wikipedia.org/wiki/ Helene_von_Breuning

Wikipedia contributors. (2023a). Jane Taylor (poet). *Wikipedia.* https://en.wikipedia.org/wiki/ Jane_Taylor_(poet)

Wikipedia contributors. (2001). Jean-Jacques Rousseau. *Wikipedia.* https://en.wikipedia.org/wiki/ Jean-Jacques_Rousseau

Hymnology: The Story Behind "Amazing Grace" – Geneva College. (n.d.). https://www.geneva. edu/blog/uncategorized/hymnology-amazing-grace#:~:text=It%20was%20December%20 1772%2C%20in,him%20out%20of%20his%20wretchedness.

Petruzzello, M. (2021, December 13). *John Newton | Biography, Conversion, Hymns, Abolition, & Facts.* Encyclopedia Britannica. https://www.britannica.com/biography/John-Newton

Wikipedia contributors. (2023f). John Newton. *Wikipedia.* https://en.m.wikipedia.org/wiki/ John_Newton

Choosing a Piano:Grand or Upright? – Musical Instrument Guide – Yamaha Corporation. (n.d.). https://www.yamaha.com/en/musical_instrument_guide/piano/selection/#:~:text=In%20 an%20upright%20piano%2C%20the,a%20greater%20potential%20for%20expression.

Bradfield Piano Restoration, Moving & Storage. (2022). Grand Piano vs. Baby Grand Piano. *Bradfield Piano Restoration, Moving & Storage.* https://bradfieldpiano.com/grand-vs-baby-grand-piano/#:~:text=Some%20piano%20manufacturers%20may%20classify,grand%20piano%20longer%20than%207%E2%80%B3.

200+ Motivational Quotes To Inspire and Win 2023. (2022, December 1). Shopify. https://www.shopify.com/blog/motivational-quotes

Liles, M. (2023, March 9). Stay Motivated When the Going Gets Tough Thanks to These 100 Quotes About Not Giving Up. Parade: Entertainment, Recipes, Health, Life, Holidays. https://parade.com/980122/marynliles/not-giving-up-quotes/

117 Never Give Up Quotes (+ My 5 Favorite Tips to Help You Keep Going). (2022, April 25). The Positivity Blog. https://www.positivityblog.com/never-give-up-quotes/

Edinburgh, K. (2023). 55 Uplifting Quotes to Encourage Making Progress. Exam Study Expert. https://examstudyexpert.com/progress-quotes/#quotes-to-help-you-get-a-new-perspective-on-your-progress

You Can Do It Quotes. (n.d.). BrainyQuote. https://www.brainyquote.com/topics/you-can-do-it-quotes

YOUR GOLDEN EARS

FIRST PIANO LESSONS

FOR ADULT BEGINNERS

Learn With 5 Minutes Daily Practice, Master Finger
Dexterity & Technique Using Sheet Music, Songs, Music
Notation and More!

VOL.2

MUSIC MOUSE STUDIOS

Contents

Introduction   ix

Your Free Gift!   xi

Join Our Community!   xii

Pacing   xiii

Focusing on Finger Dexerity   **1**

Day 120   Arpeggios   2

Day 121   Tempo Markings   4

Day 122-125   New Song: "Brahms Lullaby"   6

Day 126   About Johannes Brahms   8

Captivating Cadences   **11**

Day 127   Warmup Review   12

Day 128   Chord Progressions I IV, V, VI   13

Day 129-130   "Danny Boy" Harmonic Analysis   14

Day 131   Authentic, Plagal, Half Cadences   22

Day 132-135   New Song: "Danny Boy"   24

Stepping It Up   **29**

Day 136   Warmup Review   30

Day 137   Half Steps, Sharps, Flats, Enharmonics   31

Day 138   Half Step or Whole Step?   33

Day 139   Exercise 2   34

Day 140   Major Scale   36

Day 141   Playing and Notation Exercises   37

Unleashing Your Fingers   **39**

Day 142   16th Notes and 16th Rests   40

Day 143   Dotted 8th Notes   42

Day 144   Practice Exercises   43

Day 145	Practice Exercises	45
Day 146-149	New Song: "Prelude in C Major" (Part 1)	46
Day 150	About Johann Sebastian Bach	48
Day 151	Warmup Review	49
Day 152	Practice Exercises	50
Day 153	Practice Exercises	52
Day 154-157	New Song: "Prelude in C Major" (Part 2)	54

G Major Glory   **57**

Day 158	Key Signatures	58
Day 159	G Major Fingering	60
Day 160-161	Playing Exercises	62
Day 162-165	New Song: "Prelude in C Major" (Part 3)	65

Expressive Techniques   **67**

Day 166	Warmup Review	68
Day 167	Naturals	70
Day 168	Playing Exercises	72
Day 169	Playing Exercises	74
Day 170-173	New Song: 'Prelude in C Major" (Part 4)	76

Pedal Magic   **79**

Day 174	Warmup Review	80
Day 175-176	Chord Progressions Review	81
Day 177	Playing Exercises	84
Day 178	Improvisation	85
Day 179	Sustain Pedal	86
Day 180-185	New Song: "Prelude in C Major" – Putting It All Together	88

The Art of Articulation   **91**

Day 186	Warmup Review	92
Day 187	Order of Sharps	93
Day 188	Staccato vs. Legato	94
Day 189-192	New Song: "Minuet 3 in G Major" (Part 1)	96
Day 193	About Christian Petzold	98

Form and Function   **99**

Day 194	Warmup Review	100
Day 195	A, A'	101
Day 196	Playing Exercises	104
Day 197-200	New Song: "Minuet 3 in G Major" (Part 2)	105

Flavor of Flats   **107**

Day 201	Warmup Review	108
Day 202	Order of Flats	109
Day 203	F Major Introduction	110
Day 204	Playing an F Major Scale	111
Day 205	Playing Exercises	113
Day 206	Motifs	114
Day 207-210	New Song: "Minuet 3 in G Major" (Part 3)	115

The Grand Finale   **117**

Day 211	Warmup Review	118
Day 212	Playing Exercises	119
Day 213	B, B'	120
Day 214-218	New Song: "Minuet 3 in G Major" (Part 4)	122
Day 219	Warmup Review	123
Day 220-224	New Song: Minuet 3 in G Major by Christian Petzgold (Part 5)	124

Performance (OPTIONAL)	127
Leave A 1-Click Review!	129
Conclusion – Beyond the Last Note	131
References	133

Introduction

Mr. Reynolds, a seasoned gentleman whose weathered hands tell stories of years gone by, sits before a piano in his home, a symbol of both his aspirations and apprehensions. As Mr. Reynolds gazes at the piano keys, a whirlwind of thoughts dances behind his eyes. The passage of time has a way of casting shadows of doubt, making the prospect of learning seem like an uphill climb. With cautious determination, Mr. Reynolds lowers his hands onto the piano keys. The initial touch is hesitant, but as his fingers find their place, a melody emerges that echoes his journey. The notes are slow, but with each one played, Mr. Reynolds discovers a renewed sense of purpose, a reminder that it's never too late to embrace a new challenge. Through perseverance, the seemingly insurmountable obstacles begin to crumble. The slow pace of learning transforms into a steady rhythm of progress. The fear that once held him captive fades into the background, replaced by the sound of newfound confidence.

As the final notes resonate in the air, Mr. Reynolds lifts his gaze from the keys. A subtle smile graces his lips, a testament to the journey he has undertaken. The piano, once an enigma, has become a canvas for his expression.

Mr. Reynolds' journey mirrors that of countless others at a similar juncture. It was as if time had unraveled, revealing the uncertainties that accompany every learner, especially growing older. The weight of years and the fear of the unfamiliar can make the pace of learning feel slower. It's a reality we all share, the tinge of intimidation when we confront the unknown.

But just as Volume 1 showed us, the beauty lies in overcoming those very challenges. We've uncovered the tools to choose the right instrument, navigate the keyboard, and decipher the enigma of musical notation. Now, with Volume 2, we're equipped to venture further. We'll master strategies to strengthen finger dexterity through both exercises and songs, deepen our understanding of harmonic analysis and major scales, and explore techniques to enhance musical expression.

With this step-by-step comprehensive piano course accompanied by online demonstration videos, you can learn in digestible 5 to 30-minute lessons how to read music from well-known classical piano literature, develop finger dexterity and flexibility, gain a deep understanding of music theory, and uncover fascinating insights about the composers and songs you're learning. Written by a music veteran, Andrea Chang, the founder of Music Mouse Studios, Andrea has a dual B.A. in Music Education and Music Composition from the University of California, Los Angeles, and is an alumni of USC's prestigious Scoring for Motion Pictures and Television program. She also is a graduate of the Conservatory of Recording Arts and Sciences. Andrea has composed music and sound design, and led audio teams for video games for over a decade. She has worked on staff at Electronic Arts, Microsoft, and Hi-Rez Studios.

So, as our pianos await, let's embark on this next chapter and rewrite the narrative together. Like with any new skill, learning the piano takes time, practice, and patience. If you don't grasp it immediately, don't be discouraged - keep practicing, and you'll get there. Your unique journey deserves to be celebrated, your dreams to be nurtured. If you wish to receive further support, please visit out our website www.musicmousestudios.com for additional resources; we have a piano YouTube channel providing demonstrations and options to receive individual support. Thank you for entrusting us with your musical education - we can't wait to walk alongside you on your piano journey!

Your Free Gift!

As a token of appreciation for your support, we would like to offer you a special gift. We have curated a collection of songs and sheet music for you to explore and enjoy, featuring a variety of songs that will further enhance your piano repertoire as you continue your piano journey after the final lesson.

To receive this exclusive free download, simply visit https://www.musicmousestudios. com/contact and include the text "SHEET MUSIC" in your message. We hope these musical gems will bring you joy and inspiration. Thank you for choosing our book!

Join Our Community!

The joy of learning the piano is even greater when shared with a community of like-minded individuals. We would like to invite you to join our piano community, where you can connect with fellow pianists, share your experiences, and receive support along your musical path. Engage in inspiring conversations, exchange tips and techniques, and discover new insights from others who are on the same piano journey as you. Together, we can celebrate achievements, overcome challenges, and foster a sense of camaraderie in our shared passion for music.

To become a part of our community,
visit our website at https://www.musicmousestudios.com/community
and join us today!

Pacing

Each lesson is small, digestible, and designed to be completed within, on average, a 5-30 minute timeframe (though some lessons may take longer). If you need to review a lesson from a previous day, we encourage you to do so – repetition is key to reinforcing and solidifying your understanding of the material. If you already have some musical background, feel free to complete more than one lesson a day. This book is intended to be adaptable to learners starting at various "beginner" levels.

The goal is for each lesson to feel like a one-on-one session with a teacher, so some material will be repeated to help review and build upon the concepts you've learned from previous lessons.

Before diving into each lesson, make sure to scan the QR code below to access the accompanying instructional videos or visit https://www.musicmousestudios.com/ piano-instructional-videos. These videos will provide invaluable guidance and enhance your learning experience. So without further ado, let's get started!

LESSON
13
Focusing on Finger Dexerity

In this lesson, we will focus on strengthening our finger dexterity as we learn
how to play arpeggios in our warm-ups and new song! Let's dive in!

Arpeggios

We're going to learn how to play some arpeggios. Arpeggios consist of breaking up a chord and playing the individual notes sequentially (or "arpeggiated").

As a refresher, to form a triad (a 3-note chord), we need the 1, 3, and 5 notes of that scale.

Label the 1, 3, and 5 with the following starting notes.

1 C
   1 ___
   3 ___
   5 ___

2 G
   1 ___
   3 ___
   5 ___

3 F
   1 ___
   3 ___
   5 ___

For C (Major), the 1, 3, and 5 are C, E, and G, respectively.
For G (Major), the 1, 3, and 5 are G, B, and D, respectively.
For F (Major), the 1, 3, and 5 are F, A, and C, respectively.

First, we will play a C Major arpeggio with our left hand. Notice that it is in 3/4, meaning there are 3 beats in a measure, and the quarter note gets the beat.

☐ Write the letters below each of the notes.

☐ Play the arpeggio with the fingering provided.

Video link: https://www.musicmousestudios.com/piano-instructional-videos

Next, we will play a G Major arpeggio with our left hand.

☐ Write the letters below each of the notes.

☐ Play the arpeggio with the fingering provided.

Lastly, we will play an F Major arpeggio with our left hand.

☐ Write the letters below each of the notes.

☐ Play the arpeggio with the fingering provided.

Now that we can play these left hand arpeggios, our next song will be a breeze!

DAY 121   Tempo Markings

Here are some common tempo markings you should familiarize yourself with ("bpm" or "beats per a measure" is the same as "quarter note ="):

At the beginning of a piece, there is typically a tempo indication in the upper left of the music score. This guides the performer on the speed at which the song should be played. In "Brahm's Lullaby" (as seen in the score below), we observe the tempo marking "Andante" alongside a quarter note value of 100. "Andante" signifies a moderate, walking tempo. The quarter note = 100 indicates to set your metronome at 100 to play this piece.

Below are some frequently encountered tempo markings with their approximate metronome settings (notated in "bpm" or "beats per minute").

Larghissimo = "Very, very slowly," 20 bpm or less

Grave = "Slowly, solemnly," 20-40 bpm

Largo / Lento = "Very Slowly," 40-60 bpm

Adagio = "Slowly," 60-70 bpm

Adante = "At a Walking Pace," 70-100bpm

Moderato = "Moderately," 100-120bpm

Allegro = "Fast," 120-170bpm

Presto = "Very Fast," 170-200bpm

Prestissimo = "Extremely Fast," 200bpm+

Dynamics

Other markings you'll frequently encounter in music are dynamics, which instruct the performer on the volume at which to play the piece. In "Brahm's Lullaby," you will notice several dynamic markings such as *p, mf, f,* and *mp.*

The *p* stands for "piano," indicating to play "softly."

The *mp* stands for "mezzo-piano." "Mezzo" in Italian means "middle" or "half," implying one should play medium softly or slightly louder than *piano.*

The *f* stands for "forte," signifying to play loudly. In Italian, "forte" translates to "strong."

Similar to *mp*, *mf* stands for "mezzo-forte," instructing the performer to play "medium loud."

There are two additional markings not present in the piece but good to know.

If you come across *pp*, it stands for pianissimo, which means playing very quietly.

Conversely, *ff* denotes fortissimo, indicating to play very loudly! The suffix "issimo" in Italian serves as a superlative that means "very" or "extremely."

You may also encounter sideways "V" shaped lines resembling hairpins within the music. These are crescendo and decrescendo markings. A **crescendo** signifies a gradual increase in volume, while a **decrescendo** indicates a gradual decrease in volume.

crescendo   decrescendo

In summary,

ff = fortissimo, play very loudly

f = forte, play loudly

mf = mezzo forte, play medium loudly

mp = mezzo piano, play medium softly

p = piano, play softly

pp = pianissimo, play very softly

crescendo = gradually play louder

decrescendo = gradually play softer

New Song: "Brahms Lullaby"

☐ Write down all the letters above or below the music notes.

☐ Circle the time signature of the song. How many beats are in a measure? Which note gets the beat?

☐ Circle all the dynamics you see in the song.

Where do you play softly?

Where do you play loudly?

Where do you play medium soft?

Where do you play medium loud?

Where do you crescendo? Where do you decrescendo?

Brahm's Lullaby
for Piano

Johannes Brahms
Arranged by Andrea Chang

☐ Clap and count the rhythm of the right hand.

☐ Clap and count the rhythm of the left hand.

☐ Finger the right hand on the table. Follow the fingering provided.

☐ Finger the left hand on the table. Follow the fingering provided. Notice how these are the same arpeggios we played earlier.

☐ Finger the song with both hands on the table.

☐ Play this song slowly with your left hand first.

☐ Play this song slowly with your right hand.

☐ Play this song slowly with hands together. OPTIONAL: You can speed it up once you have mastered it.

Video link: *https://www.musicmousestudios.com/piano-instructional-videos*

DAY 126   About Johannes Brahms

Johannes Brahms was an acclaimed German composer who lived from 1833 to 1897. His compositions for orchestra, piano, voice, choir, and chamber ensembles were instrumental in defining the Romantic period music aesthetic. Initially taught by his father, Brahms displayed exceptional talent as a virtuosic pianist. At age 10, he gave his first concert, showcasing works by Beethoven and Mozart. While Brahms' family hoped he would focus on becoming a performer, to their dismay, Brahms invested much of his energy in composing. Brahms adopted the pseudonym "G. W. Marks" to conceal his identity and often wanted to destroy his earlier works, as he was very self-critical and a perfectionist.

During his career, Brahms collaborated with esteemed musicians of his time, such as the pianist Clara Schumann (wife of composer Robert Schumann) and the greatest violinist of their day, Joseph Joachim, who introduced Brahms to the Schumanns. At the age of 20, Brahms arrived at the Schumanns' doorstep, presenting Joachim's letter of recommendation to Robert Schumann. Schumann invited Brahms to play some of his works for him and was so impressed by Brahms that he published an article in his music magazine, *Neue Zeitschrift für Musik*, praising Brahms and said he was "fated to give expression to the times in the highest and most ideal manner." Brahms was overwhelmed with gratitude for the love and kindness Schumann showed him.

Schumann warmly welcomed Brahms into his home and mentored him. Unfortunately, Robert Schumann's mental health deteriorated, leading him to attempt suicide by jumping off a bridge. Though he was saved, he was subsequently confined to a psychiatric institution, where he spent the remainder of his days and ultimately died of pneumonia two years later.

Clara Schumann, Robert's wife, was prohibited from seeing him, so Brahms acted as an intermediary between the two and assisted Clara with household affairs. Brahms harbored a deep affection for Clara throughout her life, and they exchanged numerous letters over the years but never consummated their love. However, the true nature of their relationship remains unknown, as Brahms urged Clara to destroy his letters. In dedication to Clara, Brahms composed his Op. 9, the *Variations on a Theme of Schumann*.

"Brahms' Lullaby," also known as the "Cradle Song," was written for Brahms' friend Bertha Faber. Brahms first met Bertha when she sang in his women's choir in Hamburg. Although Brahms had feelings for her in her youth, they lost touch until he relocated to Vienna. By then, Bertha was married and expecting her second child, to whom Brahms composed this lullaby for. The melody originated from a Viennese song that Bertha used to sing to Brahms. Brahms wrote to Bertha's husband, stating, "Frau Bertha will realize that I wrote the 'Wiegenlied' for her little one. She will find it quite in order... that while she is singing Hans to sleep, a love song is being sung to her." The song was initially performed by Luise Dustmann on vocals, accompanied by Clara Schumann on piano.

☐ Perform "Brahms Lullaby" for someone or share it with us on our website www.music-mousestudios.com!

Congratulations, you've completed Lesson 13!

"Believe me, my journey has not been a simple journey of progress. There have been many ups and downs, and it is the choices that I made at each of those times that have helped shape what I have achieved."

—SATYA NADELLA, CEO
AND CHAIRMAN OF MICROSOFT

LESSON
14
Captivating Cadences

Our next lesson is dedicated to exploring the different ways in which music phrases or songs can come to an end. We will delve into the fascinating concept of open-ended versus closed musical cadences, which are crafted through the interplay and push and pull of various harmonies!

DAY 127   Warmup Review

☐ Play a C Major Scale with both hands ascending and descending 5 times.

☐ Play the following arpeggios in C, G, and F Major with your left hand.

☐ With your right hand, play these arpeggios in C, G, and F Major:

Video link: https://www.musicmousestudios.com/piano-instructional-videos

Chord Progressions I IV, V, VI

DAY 128

In the key of C Major, the scale's 1st, 4th, and 5th letters are C, F, and G, respectively. The 1, 4, and 5 chords, also known as I, IV, and V using Roman numerals, play a significant role in building harmonies in music. **Harmony** refers to the sequence of chords played in succession in a song. During our warm-up, we played the C, F, and G arpeggios, which, in the key of C Major, correspond to the harmonic progression of I, IV, and V.

Today, we will explore a new song called "Danny Boy," also in C Major, which utilizes the I, IV, and V chords. Additionally, it introduces a new chord, the vi (6th) chord, on A.

Each of these Roman Numeral chords has its own name. The I chord is known as the "**tonic**," the IV chord as the "**subdominant**," and the V chord as the "**dominant**." The tonic establishes the key and acts as a home base chord that the song consistently returns to. The dominant is important because it drives the harmonic progression back to the tonic. In "Danny Boy," the new chord, vi, is called the "**submediant**." The prefix "sub" means "below" or "what comes before," similar to a "subway," which is underground. Therefore, the sub-dominant (IV) comes *before* the dominant (V).

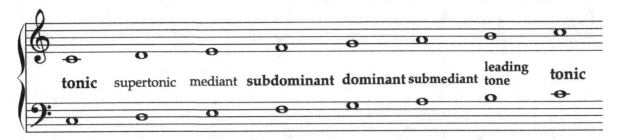

The remaining notes in the scale also have their corresponding Roman Numerals and names. The prefix "super" denotes "above," as seen in the word "superior." Hence, the "**supertonic**," which is the ii chord, is positioned "above" the tonic (I chord). The iii chord is called the "**mediant**." "Mediant" refers to the "middle" since it sits in the middle of the tonic and dominant. Similarly, the submediant, or the "lower mediant," is halfway between the dominant and leading tone, giving it its name. The vii chord, known as the "**leading tone**," leads the listener's ear back to resolution at the tonic. Familiarize yourself with these chords in the C Major scale above.

"Danny Boy" Harmonic Analysis

Danny Boy
for Piano

Traditional Irish Melody
Arranged by Andrea Chang

Identify and Play it!

1 Look at the left hand in the 2nd measure.

    a What notes are they?

    b What chord does this make?

    c What Roman numeral are they on the scale?

    d What is the name given for that Roman Numeral?

    e Use the fingering provided in the song to play these left hand chords

    Video link: *https://www.musicmousestudios.com/piano-instructional-videos*

**Answers are in the section below.

2 Look at the left hand in the 3rd measure.

    a What notes are they?

    b What chord does this make?

    c What Roman numeral are they on the scale?

    d What is the name given for that Roman Numeral?

    e Use the fingering in the song to play these left hand chords.

3 Look at the left hand in the 4th measure.

    a What notes are they?

    b What chord does this make?

    c What Roman numeral are they on the scale?

    d What is the name given for that Roman Numeral?

    e Use the fingering in the song to play these left hand chords.

4 Look at the left hand in the 5th measure.

   a What notes are they?

   b What chord does this make?

   c What Roman numeral are they on the scale?

   d What is the name given for that Roman Numeral?

   e Use the fingering in the song to play these left hand chords.

5 Look at the left hand in the 6th measure.

   a What notes are they?

   b What chord does this make?

   c What Roman numeral are they on the scale?

   d What is the name given for that Roman Numeral?

   e Use the fingering in the song to play these left hand chords.

6 Look at the left hand in the 7th measure.

   a What notes are they?

   b What chord does this make?

   c What Roman numeral are they on the scale?

   d What is the name given for that Roman Numeral?

   e Use the fingering in the song to play these left hand chords.

7 Look at the left hand in the 8th measure.

    a What notes are they?

    b What chords do they make?

    c What Roman numeral are they on the scale?

    d What is the name given for that Roman Numeral?

    e Use the fingering provided in the song to play these left hand chords.

8 Look at the left hand in the 9th measure.

    a What notes are they?

    b What chord does this make?

    c What Roman numeral are they on the scale?

    d What is the name given for that Roman Numeral?

    e Use the fingering in the song to play these left hand chords.

9 Look at the left hand in the 10th measure.

    a What notes are they?

    b What chords do they make?

    c What Roman numeral are they on the scale?

    d What is the name given for that Roman Numeral?

    e Use the fingering in the song to play these left hand chords.

10 Look at the left hand in the 11th measure.

    a   What notes are they?

    b   What chord does this make?

    c   What Roman numeral are they on the scale?

    d   What is the name given for that Roman Numeral?

    e   Use the fingering provided in the song to play these left hand chords.

11 Look at the left hand in the 12th measure.

    a   What notes are they?

    b   What chords do they make?

    c   What Roman numeral are they on the scale?

    d   What is the name given for that Roman Numeral?

    e   Use the fingering provided in the song to play these left hand chords.

12 Look at the left hand in the 13th measure.

    a   What notes are they?

    b   What chord does this make?

    c   What Roman numeral are they on the scale?

    d   What is the name given for that Roman Numeral?

    e   Use the fingering in the song to play these left hand chords.

13 Look at the left hand in the 14th and 15th measures.

   a What notes are they?

   b What chord does this make?

   c What Roman numeral are they on the scale?

   d What is the name given for that Roman Numeral?

   e Use the fingering in the song to play these left hand chords.

14 Look at the left hand in the 16th measure.

   a What notes are they?

   b What chords do they make?

   c What Roman numeral are they on the scale?

   d What is the name given for that Roman Numeral?

   e Use the fingering in the song to play these left hand chords.

15 Look at the left hand in the 17th measure.

   a What notes are they?

   b What chord does this make?

   c What Roman numeral are they on the scale?

   d What is the name given for that Roman Numeral?

   e Use the fingering provided in the song to play these left hand chords.

Answers

1 **a** C, E G, E G
   b C Major
   c I
   d Tonic

2 **a** F, C F, C F
   b F Major
   c IV
   d Subdominant

3 **a** C, E G, E G
   b C Major
   c I
   d Tonic

4 **a** G, D G, D G
   b G Major
   c V
   d Dominant

5 **a** C, E G, E G
   b C Major
   c I
   d Tonic

6 **a** F, C F, C F
   b F Major
   c IV
   d Subdominant

7 **a** C, E G, and G, D G
   b C Major, G Major
   c I, V,
   d Tonic, Dominant

8 **a** C, E G, E G
   b C Major
   c I
   d Tonic

9 **a** C, E G, and F, C F
   b C Major, F Major
   c I, IV
   d Tonic, Subdominant

10 **a** C, E G, E G
   b C Major
   c I
   d Tonic

11 **a** A, E A, and F, C F
   b A minor (we will go over this in a later lesson, so don't worry about fully understanding this at the moment), F Major
   c vi, IV
   d Submediant, Subdominant

12 **a** G, D G, D G, D G
   b G Major
   c V
   d Dominant

13 **a** C, G C and F, C F
   b C Major, F Major
   c I, IV
   d Tonic, Subdominant

14 **a** A, E A, and F, C F
   b A minor, F Major
   c vi, IV
   d submediant, subdominant

15 **a** C, G C, C G C
   b C Major
   c I
   d tonic

Authentic, Plagal, Half Cadences

Having identified all the chords in the song, we can see that the harmonic progression is organized into 2-measure long melodic phrases. Here is the harmonic progression for "Danny Boy," separated into rows for clarity:

Row 1: I, IV

Row 2: I, V

Row 3: I, IV

Row 4: I, V, I

Row 5: I IV, I

Row 6: vi, IV, V

Row 7: I, IV, I, IV

Row 8: vi, IV, I

The I, IV, and V chords are prevalent in this song's harmony. We also see patterns in the endings of the phrases, such as I IV, V I, I V I, or vi IV V. These phrase endings are called **cadences**. Here are several common cadences:

Authentic Cadence – V I
Plagal Cadence – IV I
Half Cadence – I V

An **Authentic Cadence** concludes a musical phrase by resolving from the **dominant (V) to the tonic (I)**. A **Plagal Cadence** achieves a similar resolution by moving from the **subdominant (IV) back to the tonic (I)**. A **Half Cadence**, on the other hand, does not resolve to the tonic (I) but instead leaves it unresolved on an **open-ended note with the dominant (V)**. Here are some examples in our piece, "Danny Boy," where we can see some examples of Authentic, Plagal, and Half Cadences.

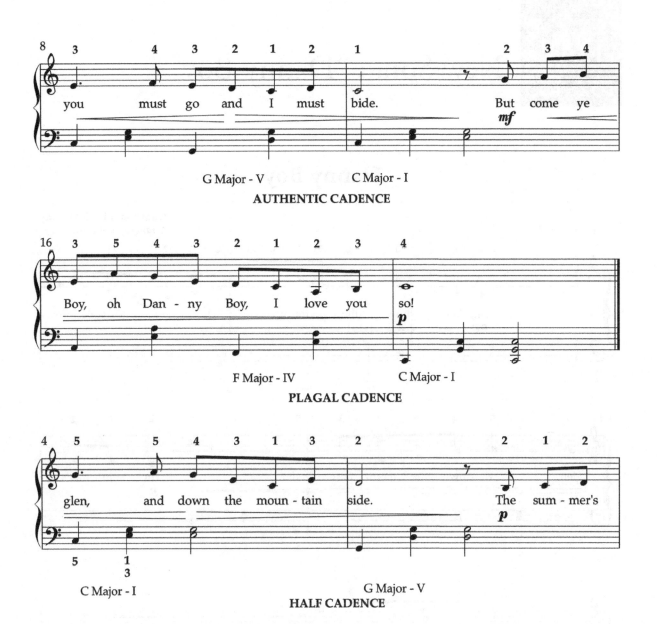

AUTHENTIC CADENCE

G Major - V   C Major - I

PLAGAL CADENCE

F Major - IV   C Major - I

HALF CADENCE

C Major - I   G Major - V

Video link: *https://www.musicmousestudios.com/piano-instructional-videos*

New Song: "Danny Boy"

Danny Boy
for Piano

Traditional Irish Melody
Arranged by Andrea Chang

Lento ♩=55

Now that we know the harmonic progression of "Danny Boy," let's try playing it.

☐ Write down all the letters above the music notes.

☐ Circle all the plagal cadences.

☐ Draw a rectangle around all the authentic cadences.

☐ Draw a triangle around all the half cadences.

☐ What is the time signature of the song?

How many beats are in a measure? Which note gets the beat?

☐ What dynamics do you see in the song?

Where do you play softly?

Where do you play loudly?

Where do you play medium soft?

Where do you play medium loud?

Where do you crescendo?

Where do you decrescendo?

☐ What is the starting tempo of the song? Lento means "slowly." What number should you set your metronome to?

Video link: https://www.musicmousestudios.com/piano-instructional-videos

☐ Clap and count the rhythm of the right hand.

☐ Clap and count the rhythm of the left hand.

☐ Finger the right hand on the table. Follow the fingering provided in the song.

☐ Finger the left hand on the table.

☐ Finger the song with both hands on the table.

☐ Play this song slowly with your left hand first.

☐ Play this song slowly with your right hand.

☐ Play this song slowly at quarter note =55 with hands together.

Congratulations, you've completed Lesson 14!

"No matter how many mistakes you make
or how slow you progress, you are still way
ahead of everyone who isn't trying."

—TONY ROBBINS

LESSON
15
Stepping It Up

In the next lesson, we'll explore various types of piano steps and how different melodic motions affect both the piano melody as well as our finger movements!

DAY 136 Warmup Review

☐ Play a C Major Scale with both hands ascending and descending 5 times.

☐ With your left hand, play these arpeggios in C, G, and F Major:

☐ With your right hand, play these arpeggios in C, G, and F Major:

Half Steps, Sharps, Flats, Enharmonics

A **half step** is the next step up or down from the current note being played, whether it's a white key or a black key. For instance, moving from C to C# (the black key next to C) is a half step. Refer to the visual below to see all of the half steps. A **sharp** (♯) denotes a half step increase up from the current note, corresponding to moving one key to the right. Conversely, a **flat** (♭) occurs when you lower the note a half step down to the left of the note.

One important consideration is that a sharp or flat only applies for the duration of the measure (if it's not a part of the key signature, which we'll discuss further).

In most cases, a half step involves transitioning from a white note to a black note, except when moving from E to F or from B to C.

In the image below, notice how the black keys on one keyboard are labeled differently from those on the other. For instance, C♯ and D♭ are different names for the same note. This is called an **enharmonic**. Likewise, F♯ and G♭ are examples of enharmonics.

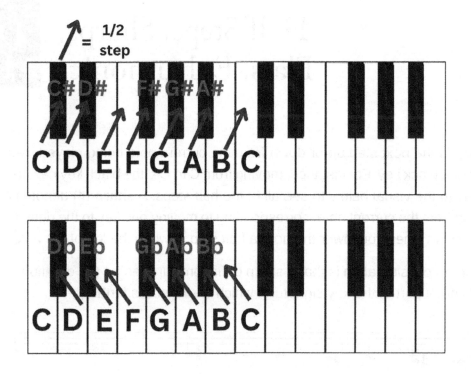

A **whole step** consists of two half steps from the current note on the piano and can be ascending or descending. The illustration below shows various examples of whole step movements on the piano. Each arrow represents a whole step.

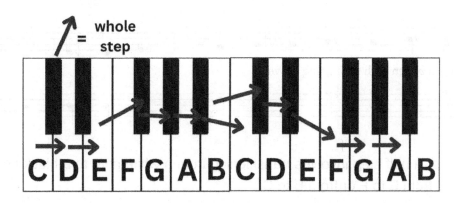

w w h w w w h

whole step between most white notes going up

whole step going up with black notes

whole step going down with black notes

Half Step or Whole Step?

Exercise 1

☐ In the exercise below, you will ascend in the **treble clef** by half steps. Please draw the note that should follow for each note provided.

☐ In the exercise below, you will ascend in the **bass clef** by half steps. Please draw the note that should follow for each note provided.

Answers

Identify if the notes on the piano are moving in half steps or whole steps.

1

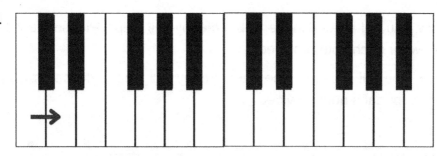

2

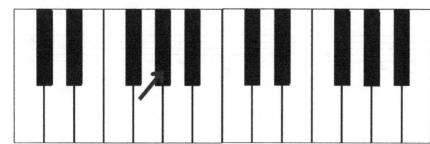

3

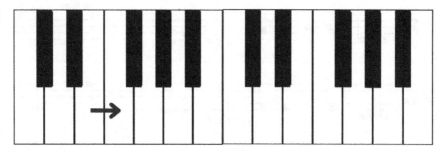

4

Answers

1 Whole step

2 Half step

3 Half step

4 Whole step

Exercise 3

☐ Identify if the notes below on the staff are moving in half steps or whole steps. If they are moving in half steps, fill in the blank with an "h." If they are moving in whole steps, fill in the blank with a "w."

Answers

DAY 140

Major Scale

A major scale follows this pattern of whole steps (w) and half steps (h):

wwh

w

wwh

or unabbreviated:

whole whole half

whole

whole whole half

Notice how the pattern consists of 2 "wwh" 's connected by a "w." This is something that you may not have realized but have already learned in previous warmups when playing a C Major scale, which follows this wwh, w, wwh pattern.

☐ Playing exercise #1: With both hands, play a C Major scale up and down **while counting the whole half pattern.**

Video link: *https://www.musicmousestudios.com/piano-instructional-videos*

Playing and Notation Exercises

☐ As a challenge, try playing a G Major scale using the whole half pattern.

Video link: *https://www.musicmousestudios.com/piano-instructional-videos*

Here is what a G Major scale looks like written on the staff with the whole half pattern. Notice how there is an F♯ written to account for the half step at the end of the pattern.

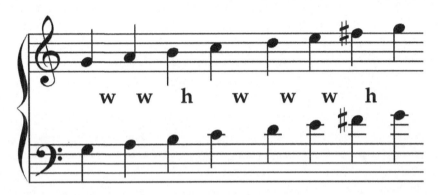

☐ Notation exercise: draw a C Major scale on the grand staff below and label all whole and half steps.

☐ Notation exercise: draw a G Major scale on the grand staff below and label all whole and half steps.

Congratulations, you've completed Lesson 15!

"You can do what you have to do, and sometimes you can do it even better than you think you can."

—JIMMY CARTER

LESSON
16
Unleashing Your Fingers

In this next lesson, we are taking it up a notch by introducing 16th notes
and applying them to a beautiful prelude composed by Bach!

16th Notes and 16th Rests

The smallest and fastest rhythmic unit we've covered in the rhythm tree so far has been 8th notes. We can extend this even further by cutting 8th notes in half, and as a result, we have 16th notes. There are four 16th notes in a beat and sixteen 16th notes in a whole note, hence its name. The same applies to cutting 8th rests in half, which results in 16th rests. Similarly, there are four 16th rests in a beat and sixteen 16th rests in a whole rest.

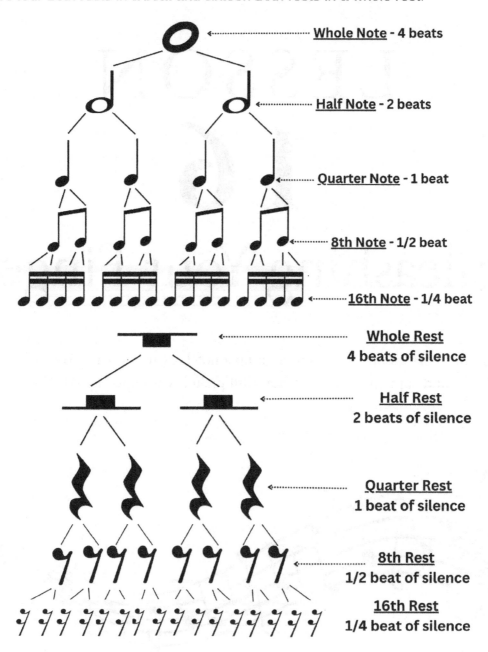

Whole Note - 4 beats

Half Note - 2 beats

Quarter Note - 1 beat

8th Note - 1/2 beat

16th Note - 1/4 beat

Whole Rest
4 beats of silence

Half Rest
2 beats of silence

Quarter Rest
1 beat of silence

8th Rest
1/2 beat of silence

16th Rest
1/4 beat of silence

To count 16th notes, it is similar to 8th notes where we have "1 & 2 &...," but we fill in the extra notes in between with an "a" and say, "one a and a."

counting with 8th notes   **counting with 16th notes**

1 & 2 & 3 & 4 &   1 a & a 2 a & a 3 a & a 4 a & a

☐ Clap through the extended rhythm tree with the 16th notes.

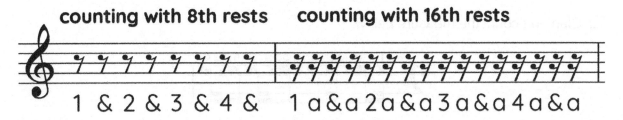

counting with 8th rests   **counting with 16th rests**

1 & 2 & 3 & 4 &   1 a & a 2 a & a 3 a & a 4 a & a

☐ "Clap" through the extended rests tree with the 16th rests.

Video link: https://www.musicmousestudios.com/piano-instructional-videos

Dotted 8th Notes

Similar to how dotted quarter notes are often followed by an 8th note, dotted 8th notes are often followed by a 16th note.

A dotted 8th note is the same as an 8th note + a 16th note, so when counting, we must allot out three 16th note beats to them.

☐ Clap and count the measure below.

Video link: https://www.musicmousestudios.com/piano-instructional-videos

Rhythm Exercises

☐ Practice Exercise #1 – Clap and count the rhythm below. Notice how we start with an 8th rest, which is the same as two 16th rests or "1a." Then we start clapping on the "&a" of the first and 3rd beats.

☐ Practice Exercise #2 – Clap and count the rhythm below. Notice how we start with a 16th note followed by a dotted 8th note, which is then tied to a quarter note. Remember that when there is a tie, you hold the note across the duration of all the notes in the tie (so you would only play on "1," "a" of 1, "3," and "a" of 3).

Video link: https://www.musicmousestudios.com/piano-instructional-videos

☐ Practice Exercise #3 – Let's take the rhythm from Exercise 1 and apply them to some notes! Play the following exercise. Write down the letter notes if needed. Please use the fingering provided. Also, note the dynamics and practice incorporating them into your playing.

> **Tip 1:** While practicing these exercises, try to rotate your wrist towards the high E every time you play it. This technique will enhance the connection between your fingers, creating smoother and more fluid movements and sounds. Keep your fingers and hands loose and allow them to flow in the direction of the notes.

> **Tip 2**: Please note that the fingering provided is merely a suggestion. If you find it more comfortable to use different fingers for certain notes, feel free to make adjustments according to your preference and ease of playing.

> *Video link: https://www.musicmousestudios.com/piano-instructional-videos*

Play the rest of the exercises below with the appropriate rhythm, fingering, and dynamics. Write down the letter notes if needed.

☐ Practice Exercise #4

☐ Practice Exercise #5

☐ Practice Exercise #6

☐ Practice Exercise #7

Play the rest of the exercises below with the appropriate rhythm, fingering, and dynamics. Write down the letter notes if needed.

Video link: https://www.musicmousestudios.com/piano-instructional-videos

☐ Practice Exercise #8

☐ Practice Exercise #9

☐ Practice Exercise #10 – **Play this with your left hand.** Notice that we hold both the C while playing the E right after it. This rhythm is the same as in Practice Exercise #2, except you hold the first note for the entire duration.

☐ Practice Exercise #11

New Song:
"Prelude in C Major" (Part 1)

Most of the songs we've looked at so far have been in C Major (using all of the white keys). Though C Major doesn't naturally contain any sharps or flats, we can still have pieces in C Major that add sharps and flats in various measures, such as in Johann Sebastian Bach's "Prelude in C Major."

In this piece, the right hand plays arpeggios most of the time while the left hand keeps it steady with a bass line. You will also feel the tension, the push and pull between chords in this song, which is caused by the harmonic progression and the need for notes to resolve back to the tonic. We won't analyze the harmony here like in "Danny Boy," but that is an excellent exercise if you want a challenge!

Since this song is a bit longer, we will break it into 4 sections to learn throughout the next several lessons.

In measure 1, "*simile*" means "similar," indicating that you should play beats 3-4 in a similar way to beats 1-2. This mainly refers to using the same fingering, but if you look at the notes in beats 1-2, they are exactly the same as the notes in beats 3-4.

☐ Write down all the letters above or below the music notes.

☐ Circle all the places where you play **p**.

☐ Circle all the places where you play **f**.

☐ Circle all the places where you play **pp**.

☐ What measure do you crescendo?

☐ What measure do you decrescendo?

☐ What is the time signature of the piece? How many beats per measure are there, and what note gets the beat?

Video link: *https://www.musicmousestudios.com/piano-instructional-videos*

☐ Clap and count the rhythm of the right hand. Notice how every single measure has the same rhythm.

☐ Clap and count the rhythm of the left hand. Notice how every single measure has the same rhythm.

☐ Finger the right hand on the table. Follow the fingering provided.

☐ Finger the left hand on the table. Follow the fingering provided.

☐ Finger the song with both hands on the table.

☐ Play this song slowly with your right hand first.

☐ Play this song slowly with your left hand.

☐ Play this song slowly with hands together.

Prelude in C Major
from The Well-Tempered Clavier

Johann Sebastian Bach

DAY 150

About Johann Sebastian Bach

Johannes Sebastian Bach, one of the greatest composers of all time, lived from 1685 to 1750 and wrote "Prelude in C Major." He was a German composer born into a musical family, with his father being a city musician and his eldest brother an organist. Bach was the youngest of eight children, coming from a lineage of composers. Tragically, he became an orphan at the age of 10 when both his mother and father passed away within eight months of each other. He then lived with his eldest brother, Johann Christoph Bach, who was fourteen years his senior, for 5 years.

Bach worked as a musician for Protestant churches, which influenced his compositions for organ and chamber music. He had a pattern of conflicts with authority figures, such as expressing dissatisfaction with the quality of singers in his choir and receiving a reprimand after calling one of his students a "weenie bassoonist." This student then hit Bach with a stick. Bach also faced consequences for informing his employer he would be gone for 4 weeks but instead traveled for 4 months. Bach later took on a job as a court organist but fell out of favor with his employer and ended up being dismissed and subsequently imprisoned. His discharge from jail was also unfavorable, as he too stubbornly pressed for his dismissal. However, he later received the honor of "Royal Court Composer" from the king of Poland, Augustus III.

Bach's extensive and diverse musical output encompassed 215 cantatas, preludes, fugues, motets, passions, chorales, sacred music, chamber music, and concertos. He was renowned for his mastery of counterpoint and his ability to develop musical motifs in his compositions. One of Bach's famous works, *The Well-Tempered Clavier*, consists of two books with 24 preludes and fugues each, written in every major and minor key. Our "Prelude in C Major" is part of this collection.

Bach was fruitful and prolific in both his compositions as well as his offspring. He married twice, with his first marriage to his second cousin, Maria Barbara Bach, resulting in seven children, although three died at a young age. Bach further experienced a tragic loss when

he returned from a trip one day only to find that Maria, 35 years old and healthy at the time, had unexpectedly died and had been buried in his absence. The cause of her death is not documented. The following year, Bach met Anna Magdalena, a talented soprano whom he married. They had a total of 13 children, but only six survived into adulthood. Anna Magdalena, a talented musician herself, together with her husband, was able to run a household with servants and students in which music supported their entire family.

☐ Play a C Major Scale with both hands ascending and descending 5 times.

☐ Try playing the C Major arpeggio with both hands together:

Video link: *https://www.musicmousestudios.com/piano-instructional-videos*

DAY 152 — Practice Exercises

☐ **Practice Exercise #1 (Review)** – Clap and count the rhythm below.

☐ **Practice Exercise #2 (Review)** – Clap and count the rhythm below.

Play the following exercises with the appropriate rhythm, fingering, and dynamics. Write down the letter notes if needed.

☐ **Practice Exercise #3** – Notice the sharp starting on the second note.

Video link: https://www.musicmousestudios.com/piano-instructional-videos

☐ **Practice Exercise #4**

☐ Practice Exercise #5 – Notice the sharp starting on the third note.

☐ Practice Exercise #6

☐ Practice Exercise #7

DAY 153

Practice Exercises

Play the following exercises with the appropriate rhythm, fingering, and dynamics. Write down the letters on top of the notes if needed.

Video link: https://www.musicmousestudios.com/piano-instructional-videos

☐ Practice Exercise #8

☐ Practice Exercise #9

☐ Practice Exercise #10

☐ Practice Exercise #11 – Play this with your left hand.

☐ Practice Exercise #12 – Play this with your left hand.

☐ Practice Exercise #13 – Play this with your left hand.

☐ Write down all the letters above or below the music notes.

☐ Circle all the places where you play *p*.

☐ Circle all the places where you play *pp*.

☐ What measure(s) do you crescendo?

☐ What measure do you decrescendo?

☐ What sharp is in measure 10?

Remember, this sharp carries across the whole measure.

☐ What sharp is in measure 12?

Remember, this sharp carries across the whole measure.

Video link: https://www.musicmousestudios.com/piano-instructional-videos

☐ Clap and count the rhythm of the right hand. Notice how every single measure has the same rhythm.

☐ Clap and count the rhythm of the left hand. Notice how every single measure has the same rhythm.

☐ Finger the right hand on the table. Follow the fingering provided.

☐ Finger the left hand on the table. Follow the fingering provided.

☐ Finger the song with both hands on the table.

☐ Play this song slowly with your right hand first.

☐ Play this song slowly with your left hand.

☐ Play this song slowly with hands together.

Congratulations, you've completed Lesson 16!

"Never say never, because limits,
like fears, are often just an illusion."

—MICHAEL JORDAN

LESSON
17
G Major Glory

Let's explore G Major in its full glory!

DAY 158 Key Signatures

A key signature is a series of sharps or flats displayed at the beginning of a piece of music, following the clef symbol. It indicates which black keys must be played consistently throughout the entire song. These sharps or flats apply to every measure, meaning that if, for instance, there is an F♯ in the key signature, every occurrence of the note F in the song will be played as F♯.

G Major Introduction

In the key signature of G Major, the note F is represented as F♯, as mentioned earlier. Here is how it appears when written on the staff.

Observe how F♯ is written on the top line F in the treble clef since the line notes in the treble clef are EGBDF ("Every Good Boy Does Fine"), with F being the top line note. Similarly, in the bass clef, we can find the F that we want to sharpen by remembering that the line notes from bottom to top are GBDFA ("Good Boys Do Fine Always").

When drawing the key signature, ensure that the middle portion of the sharp symbol is on the F line, similar to how you draw a circle for a whole note. Take a moment to draw the G Major key signature on the staff provided.

Now, let's locate F♯ on the piano. Begin by finding the note F, then move to the next black key to the right of it.

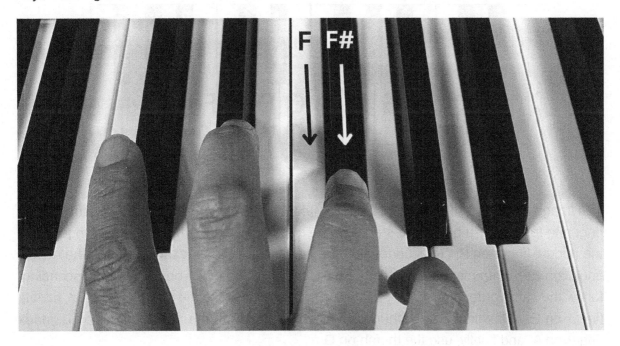

Video link: *https://www.musicmousestudios.com/piano-instructional-videos*

DAY 159

G Major Fingering

In today's lesson, we will focus on playing a G Major scale. As a reminder, a Major scale follows the pattern of:

whole step, whole step, half step,

whole step,

whole step, whole step, half step.

Applying this pattern to the starting note G, we get the notes G, A, B, C, D, E, F♯, and G, which is why the key signature of G Major contains one sharp, which is F♯.

The image above displays the notes of a G Major scale on the piano and the recommended fingering for the **right hand**. We start with the right thumb on G, then the index finger on A, the middle finger on B, cross under with the thumb to C, the index finger on D, the middle finger on E, the ring finger on F♯, and finally end with the pinky on G. When descending, follow the same order in reverse: start with the pinky on G, use the ring finger on F♯, middle finger on E, index finger on D, thumb on C, cross over with the middle finger on B, index finger on A, and finally, use the thumb on G.

For left hand fingering, refer to the visual below.

Left hand fingering

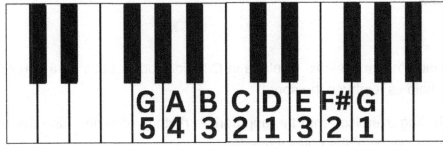

When ascending with the left hand, begin with the pinky on G, proceed to the ring finger on A, middle finger on B, the index finger on C, thumb on D, cross over with the middle finger to E, use the index finger for F♯, and finally, reach the top note G with the thumb. When descending, follow the reverse order: start with the thumb on G, move to the index finger on F♯, middle finger for E, cross under with the thumb to play D, continue with the index finger on C, the middle finger on B, the ring finger on A, and the pinky for G.

Warmup

☐ Play an ascending and descending G Major Scale with your right hand 5 times.

☐ Play an ascending and descending G Major Scale with your left hand 5 times.

☐ Play an ascending and descending G Major Scale with both hands together 5 times.

Video link: https://www.musicmousestudios.com/piano-instructional-videos

DAY 160-161   Playing Exercises

We will continue to learn Bach's "Prelude in C Major" today. Let's do a couple of playing exercises to help us reinforce the song!

Play the following exercises with the appropriate rhythm, fingering, and dynamics. Write down the letters on top of the notes if needed.

Video link: *https://www.musicmousestudios.com/piano-instructional-videos*

☐ Practice Exercise #1

☐ Practice Exercise #2 – Note the flat on the first note.

☐ Practice Exercise #3

☐ Practice Exercise #4 – Note the flat on the third note.

☐ Practice Exercise #5 – Observe the flat on the third note.

☐ Practice Exercise #6

☐ Practice Exercise #7

☐ Practice Exercise #8

☐ Practice Exercise #9

☐ Practice Exercise #10 – Use your left hand for this exercise.

☐ Practice Exercise #11 – Watch out for all the sharps and flats. Use your left hand for this exercise.

☐ Practice Exercise #12 – Use your left hand for this exercise.

☐ Write down all the letters above or below the music notes (this is optional).

☐ What measure(s) do you crescendo?

☐ What measure(s) do you decrescendo?

☐ What measure do you play *pp*?

☐ What flat is in measure 20? Remember that every time you see a B in this measure, it is flat.

☐ What sharps and flats do you see in measure 22? Remember, both the sharp and the flat carry across the full measure.

☐ What flats do you see in measures 23-24?

☐ Clap and count the rhythm of the right hand. Notice how every single measure has the same rhythm.

☐ Clap and count the rhythm of the left hand. Notice how every single measure has the same rhythm.

☐ Finger the right hand on the table. Follow the fingering provided.

☐ Finger the left hand on the table. Follow the fingering provided.

☐ Finger the song with both hands on the table.

☐ Play this song slowly with your right hand first.

☐ Play this song slowly with your left hand.

☐ Play this song slowly with hands together.

Video link: https://www.musicmousestudios.com/piano-instructional-videos

Congratulations, you've completed Lesson 17!

"It does not matter how slowly you
go as long as you do not stop."

—CONFUCIUS

LESSON
18
Expressive Techniques

Music is not music without emotion! In this lesson, we will explore
diverse chords and notes that infuse our music with flavor. Additionally,
we will investigate various tempo modifiers that enhance expression
and evoke a sense of drama in our musical performances!

DAY 166

Warmup Review

☐ Play an ascending and descending C Major Scale with both hands 5 times.

☐ Play an ascending and descending G Major Scale with both hands 5 times.

Dominant 7th Chord

Today, we're going to be learning what a dominant 7th chord is. Previously, we discussed the dominant chord as being built on a triad with the 1, 3, and 5 notes on a scale. A dominant 7th chord takes this triad and adds another 3rd on top, specifically the 7th note of the scale (hence the name "Dominant 7th"). Therefore, a dominant 7th chord consists of the 1st, 3rd, 5th, and 7th notes of the scale.

This 7th is lowered by a half step (making it a minor 7th instead of a major 7th chord). Taking a C dominant 7th chord as an example, the natural 7th note of C Major is B. However, a C Dominant 7th chord will lower that B by a half step to a B♭, with the notes of the C Dominant 7th chord being C, E, G, B♭. Dominant 7ths can help add more flavor to a piece of music and creates an even stronger desire to resolve to the tonic with the flat 7th.

Let's consider another example with the G dominant 7th chord, consisting of the notes G, B, D, and F (the F is lowered by a half step from F♯).

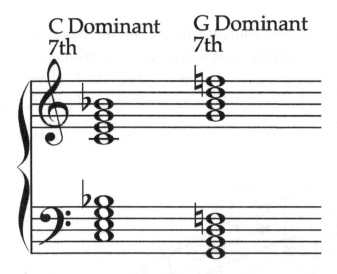

Video link: https://www.musicmousestudios.com/piano-instructional-videos

Like other triads, dominant 7th chords can also be played in different inversions and may have missing notes, which is typical. However, the 7th note will always be included to imply that it is a dominant 7th chord.

Although we will not cover the specific inversions of dominant 7th chords at this time, it is important to note that they exist and function similarly to the inversions of triads. Any of the notes in a dominant 7th chord can be the bottom note, and the notes within the chord can be arranged in different orders.

DAY 167 Naturals

In the G dominant 7th chord, you might notice a symbol preceding the F. This symbol is called a **natural** sign, which instructs the performer to play the regular white note instead of any sharps or flats played previously or indicated by the key signature.

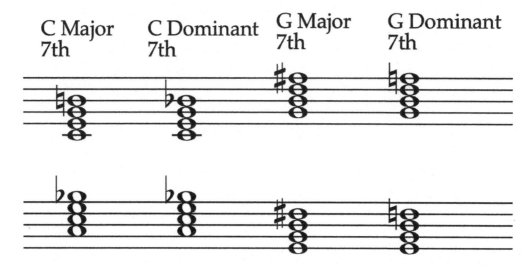

In the case of the G dominant 7th chord, instead of playing the F♯ typically found in G Major (as shown in the regular G Major 7th chord below), we play an F♮ in the G Dominant 7th chord. Similarly, in the C dominant 7th chord, rather than playing the usual B♮ in a C Major 7th chord, we lower it by a half step to a B♭.

Ritardando

Ritardando is a tempo marking in music that instructs the performer to gradually slow down the pace. This often occurs at the end of the piece, section, or at the conclusion of a phrase to enhance the sense of drama and provide a sense of finality. In the song we're playing today, you will see the tempo marking "*poco rit.*" "Poco" in Italian means "little," and "rit." is an abbreviation for "ritardando." So "*poco rit.*" means to slow down a little bit.

Fermata

A **fermata** is a notation symbol that indicates that a note or a chord should be held longer than its written value.

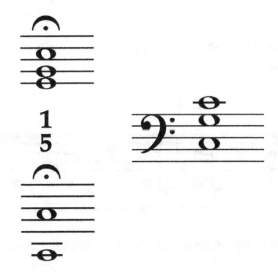

The performer has the freedom to determine the length of the pause. Like ritardando, fermatas are typically found at the end of a piece, phrase, or section to provide a sense of conclusion. There will be a fermata in the next music section we'll be playing. The fermata symbol resembles a bird's eye and is placed above the note or chord it affects.

Practice drawing a fermata on the bass clef C chord above.

Playing Exercises

We will be finishing up Bach's Prelude in C Major today! Let's do a couple of playing exercises to help us finish strong!

Theory Exercise #1 – Look at the notes in the measure above. List out what the notes are.

Theory Exercise #2 – If we're in the key of C Major, what chord does this make?

The notes G, B, and F imply a G Dominant 7th chord. Considering that this song is in C Major, a G Dominant 7th chord is fitting because G is the 5th, or dominant, in the C Major scale.

Play the following exercises with the appropriate rhythm, fingering, and dynamics. Write down the letters notes if needed.

Video link*: https://www.musicmousestudios.com/piano-instructional-videos*

Practice Exercise #1

☐ Practice Exercise #2 – Pay attention to the sharp on the third note.

☐ Practice Exercise #3

☐ Practice Exercise #4

☐ Practice Exercise #5 – Pay attention to the flat on the second note.

Video link: https://www.musicmousestudios.com/piano-instructional-videos

☐ Practice Exercise #6 – Pay attention to the fourth finger movement. Play this slowly and follow the fingering provided.

☐ Practice Exercise #7 – Use your **right hand** for this exercise. Play this slowly and follow the fingering provided.

☐ Practice Exercise #8 – Use your **left hand** for this exercise.

☐ Practice Exercise #9 – Use your **left hand** for this exercise.

☐ Practice Exercise #10 – Use your **left hand** for this exercise.

☐ Write down all the letters above or below the music notes (optional).

☐ What is the name of the chord in measure 28?

☐ What other measure do you see with a dominant 7th chord?

☐ What measure(s) do you crescendo?

☐ What measure(s) do you decrescendo?

☐ What measure do you play *f*?

☐ What measure do you play *p*?

☐ What flats and sharps are in measure 29? Remember that these carry throughout the measure.

- [ ] What sign do you see in measure 30?
- [ ] What flats do you see in measure 33? Remember that these flats persist throughout the measure.
- [ ] In measure 34, what clef is the right hand playing in? What clef is the left hand playing in?

Notice how they are both in the same clef since the notes that the right hand plays are very low and best notated with a bass clef rather than a treble clef.

- [ ] In measure 35, what note do you start to slow down playing a little bit on?
- [ ] What symbol do you see in the last measure in both the right and left hands?
- [ ] Clap and count the rhythm of the right hand. Notice how every measure has the same rhythm except for the last one.
- [ ] Clap and count the rhythm of the left hand. Notice how every measure has the same rhythm except for the last one.
- [ ] Finger the right hand on the table. Follow the fingering provided.
- [ ] Finger the left hand on the table. Follow the fingering provided.
- [ ] Finger the song with both hands on the table.
- [ ] Play this song slowly with your right hand first.
- [ ] Play this song slowly with your left hand.
- [ ] Play this song slowly with hands together.

Video link: https://www.musicmousestudios.com/piano-instructional-videos

Congratulations, you've completed Lesson 18!

"Character consists of what you do on the third and fourth tries."

—JAMES A. MICHENER

LESSON
19
Pedal Magic

Now… for the icing on the cake… we will learn the art of using the pedal to seamlessly blend all the notes together, resulting in a serene musical landscape!

Warmup Review

☐ Play a C Major Scale with both hands ascending and descending 5 times.

☐ Play a G Major Scale with both hands ascending and descending 5 times.

☐ Play a C Major Arpeggio with both hands.

☐ Play a G Major Arpeggio with both hands. Notice how in the right hand, the notes are an octave lower.

☐ Play an F Major Arpeggio with both hands. Notice how in the right hand, the notes are an octave lower.

Video link: https://www.musicmousestudios.com/piano-instructional-videos

Chord Progressions Review

1 What key is the chord progression below in?

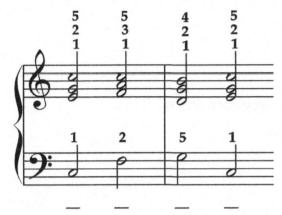

2 Label the Roman Numerals for the chord progression above.

3 What key is the chord progression below in?

4 Label the Roman Numerals for the chord progression above.

5 What key is the chord progression below in?

6 Label the Roman Numerals for the chord progression above.

7 What key is the chord progression below in?

8 Label the Roman Numerals for the chord progression above.

Answers

1 C Major

2

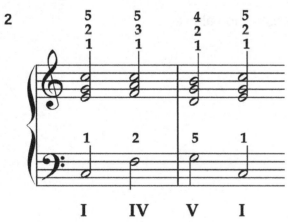

I   IV   V   I

3 C Major

4

vi   IV   V   I

5 G Major

6

I   IV   V   I

7 G Major

8

vi   IV   V   I

DAY 177

Playing Exercises

Try playing the chord progressions from the previous exercises and use the fingering provided.

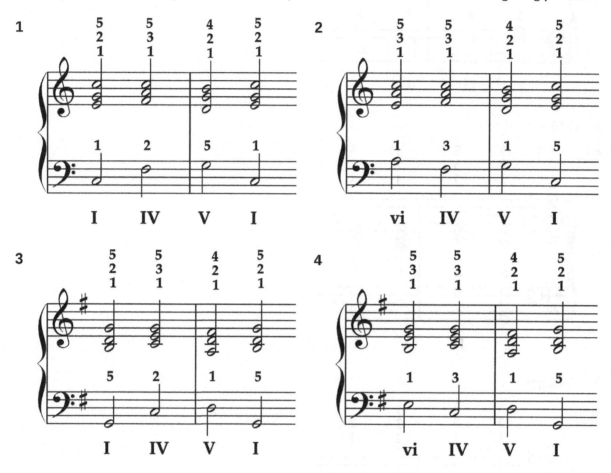

Video link: *https://www.musicmousestudios.com/piano-instructional-videos*

Choose one of the chord progressions above and play the bass clef notes with your left hand. With your right hand, play any of the notes in a C Major scale in any order to make up your own melody!

Video link: https://www.musicmousestudios.com/piano-instructional-videos

DAY 179

Sustain Pedal

The sustain pedal, located at the bottom of the piano or keyboard, is used to sustain the notes played on the piano, ensuring a smooth and connected sound.

On an acoustic piano, the pedal on the right is the sustain pedal. When using a sustain pedal, make sure that the heel of your foot is placed firmly on the ground and that your toe is facing upward.

On a keyboard, there is generally just one electric pedal, but the same rule of thumb applies – ensure that the heel of your foot is placed firmly on the ground and your toe is facing upward, and then press down.

The timing of applying the sustain pedal is crucial for achieving that smooth and connected sound in your piano playing. The pedal should be pressed immediately **after** changing a chord or measure, ensuring that it catches the note while you're still holding the keys down. It's important to *slightly delay your foot* pressing the pedal after your fingers press the keys. This creates an overlap, allowing the sound to sustain either through the notes held down by your fingers or by the sustain pedal operated by your foot.

Let's apply the pedal to the "Prelude in C Major" piece that we've been practicing. Try pushing down the sustain pedal right *after* the 16th rest in the left hand (so, for example, we should be pushing the pedal down right when we play that left hand E in the first measure). The second time you should press the pedal down would be after the 16th rest on beat 3, on that second E in the left hand.

Prelude in C Major

from The Well-Tempered Clavier

Johann Sebastian Bach

Try out the sustain pedal on that first row of 3 measures. Starting with measure 1, play the middle C with your left hand. Then immediately, as you're playing the E that follows, push down the sustain pedal and hold it through until **right after** you play that middle C again with your left hand on beat 1 of measure 2 and then lift the sustain pedal quickly and then push it down again so that the sustain pedal lands right at the same time with the D. Then you will do the same thing and hold the sustain pedal down through the first beat of measure 3 (through the B below middle C) and right after playing that note, lift the sustain pedal quickly and put it back down again on that D that follows the B after beat 1 on the "a." Essentially, the sustain pedal will always lag behind that first note held down by your fingers ever so slightly but then the pedal will be down and sustaining that note when your fingers lift up from it and go to the second note. It's this overlap that helps to create that long, sustained line. Refer to the video to hear it in action.

Video link: https://www.musicmousestudios.com/piano-instructional-videos

Let's apply the sustain pedal to the rest of Bach's "Prelude in C Major."

DAY 180-185

New Song: "Prelude in C Major" – Putting It All Together

Prelude in C Major

from The Well-Tempered Clavier

Johann Sebastian Bach

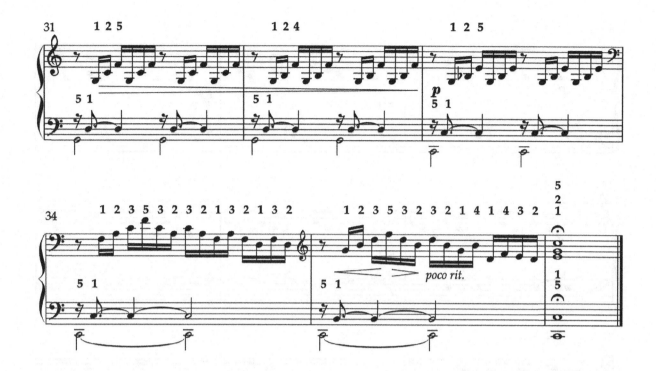

Now you know all of the sections that make up this piece. We are going to put it all together now!

☐ Play this song slowly with your right hand first.

☐ Play this song slowly with your left hand.

☐ Play this song slowly with hands together.

☐ Add the sustain pedal.

☐ Practice until you feel confident with it!

☐ Perform this song for someone you know!

Video link: https://www.musicmousestudios.com/piano-instructional-videos

Congratulations, you've completed Lesson 19!

"You've got to get up every morning
with determination if you're going
to go to bed with satisfaction."

—GEORGE LORIMER

LESSON
20
The Art of
Articulation

Punctuation, emphasis, pacing, melodic motion – we will tackle these
and more as we master the art of articulation in the next lesson!

DAY 186   Warmup Review

☐ Play an ascending and descending C Major Scale with both hands 5 times.

☐ Play an ascending and descending G Major Scale with both hands 5 times.

☐ Play a C Major Arpeggio with both hands.

☐ Play a G Major Arpeggio with both hands.

☐ Play an F Major Arpeggio with both hands.

The order of sharps is a specific sequence of sharps used to determine the key signature. The order is as follows: F♯, C♯, G♯, D♯, A♯, E♯, B♯. How do we apply the order of sharps?

If a key signature has 1 sharp, it will be F♯, as it is the first sharp in the order. If a key signature has 2 sharps, it will be F♯ and C♯, the first two sharps in the sequence. Similarly, for 3 sharps, the key signature will be F♯, C♯, and G♯, following the first three sharps in the order, and so on.

Now let's take that previous example of a key signature having 3 sharps F♯ C♯ G♯. How do we determine the key signature from these 3 sharps? The rule of thumb here is to **take the last sharp (G♯ in this case) and raise it up by a half step** to determine the key that you're in. So a half step up from G♯ is A Major. Therefore, the key of A Major has F♯ C♯ G♯ in it.

Let's Practice!

See if you can answer the questions below:

1 If a key signature has 2 sharps, what are the sharps?

2 What key would we be in?

3 If a key signature has 4 sharps, what are the sharps?

4 What key would we be in?

5 If a key signature has 5 sharps, what are the sharps?

6 What key would we be in?

7 If a key signature has 7 sharps, what are the sharps?

8 What key would we be in?

Answers

1 F♯ C♯

2 D Major

3 F♯ C♯ G♯ D♯

4 E Major

5 F♯ C♯ G♯ D♯ A♯

6 B Major

7 F♯ C♯ G♯ D♯ A♯ E♯ B♯

8 C♯ Major

DAY 188

Staccato vs. Legato

Staccato is an articulation marking used to indicate which notes should be played in a short and detached manner. It is represented by a small dot placed above the notes. **Legato** is the opposite of staccato and refers to playing notes smoothly and connected without noticeable breaks between them. In some cases, legato is indicated by a slur marking, but often it is the default way of playing unless specified otherwise.

Play the exercises below. The first note of each measure should be played legato, followed by 2 staccato notes on G (played first by the thumb and then by the index finger the second time around).

Video link: https://www.musicmousestudios.com/piano-instructional-videos

Parallel Motion

Parallel motion refers to the simultaneous movement of two hands playing notes in the same direction. We observe parallel motion in our warm-ups as we play ascending and descending scales.

In the example below, notice how this simultaneous upward movement of both hands demonstrates parallel motion.

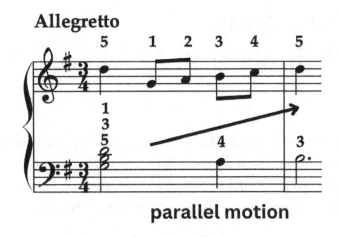

parallel motion

☐ Play the above exercise with your right hand alone.

☐ Play the above exercise with your left hand alone.

☐ Play the above exercise with both hands. Feel the parallel motion in your hands as they move in the same direction.

Video link: *https://www.musicmousestudios.com/piano-instructional-videos*

Contrary Motion

On the contrary, **contrary motion** is the opposite of parallel motion, where the hands play and move in opposite directions. In the example below, the left hand notes move to the left while the right hand notes simultaneously move to the right, exemplifying contrary motion.

☐ Play the above exercise with right hand alone.

☐ Play the above exercise with left hand alone.

☐ Play the above exercise with both hands. Feel the contrary motion in your hands as they move in the opposite direction.

contrary motion

Video link: *https://www.musicmousestudios.com/piano-instructional-videos*

DAY 189-192

New Song: "Minuet 3 in G Major" (Part 1)

Today we will start a new song called "Minuet 3" in G Major by Christian Petzgold! We will be learning this song throughout the next several lessons. The tempo marking is "Allegretto," which indicates a moderately fast pace. The term "Allegretto" contains the Italian diminutive "-etto," meaning "little," suggesting a slightly slower tempo than the standard "Allegro."

Minuet 3
in G Major

Christian Petzgold
Minuet from the "Notebook for Anna Magedalena Bach"

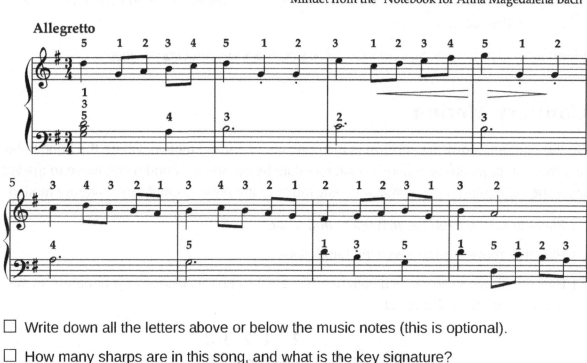

☐ Write down all the letters above or below the music notes (this is optional).

☐ How many sharps are in this song, and what is the key signature?

☐ How many beats are there in a measure?

☐ What measure do you crescendo?

☐ What measure do you decrescendo?

☐ In measure 1, what interval do we see in the right hand from beat 1 to beat 2 (from D to G)?

☐ In measure 2, what interval do you see in the right hand from beat 1 to beat 2 (from D to G)?

- [ ] In measure 3, what interval do you see in the right hand from beat 1 to beat 2 (from E to C)?

- [ ] In measure 4, what interval do you see in the right hand from beat 1 to beat 2 (from G to G)?

- [ ] In measure 7, what intervals do you see in the left hand (from D to B, B to G)?

- [ ] In measure 8, what interval do you see in the left hand from beat 1 to 2 (from D to D)? What about from beat 2 to 2& (D to C)?

- [ ] Point to all the areas where there is stepwise motion (going up or down the scale by 2nds).

The melody in the right hand consists of a combination of leaps and steps. In measure 1, there is a 5th interval between the first and the second note (D to G). Then, we continue with stepwise motion up the scale until the second measure, where another 5th leap occurs from D to G. Moving to measure 3, the first beat starts with a downward leap of a 3rd, followed by an upward stepwise motion leading into the 4th measure. In measure 4, we encounter the largest leap yet of an octave down from G to G. The remaining section predominantly consists of stepwise motion for the right hand. In contrast, the left hand exhibits downward leaps in 3rds in the seventh measure and an octave leap below in the eighth measure.

- [ ] Circle all the staccato notes.

- [ ] Clap and count the rhythm of the right hand. Notice how the rhythm in measures 1-2 is the same as in measures 3-4. Measures 5, 6, and 7 also have the same rhythm.

- [ ] Clap and count the rhythm of the left hand. How many dotted half notes do you see? (There should be 5).

- [ ] Finger the right hand on the table. Follow the fingering provided in the song.

- [ ] Finger the left hand on the table. Follow the fingering provided in the song.

- [ ] Finger the song with both hands on the table.

- [ ] Play this song slowly with your right hand first.

- [ ] Play this song slowly with your left hand.

- [ ] Play this song slowly with hands together.

Video link: *https://www.musicmousestudios.com/piano-instructional-videos*

About Christian Petzold

Christian Petzold, a German composer and organist, lived from 1677 to 1733 and held the position of court chamber composer in 1709. While only a few of his works have survived, the "Minuet in G Major" we are currently learning is one of them. This piece was preserved in the *Notebook for Anna Magdalena Bach* (Anna Magdalena being the second wife of Johann Sebastian Bach).

Petzold's "Minuet in G Major" and his "Minuet in G Minor" are well-known pieces featured in the notebook. Initially, these compositions were mistakenly attributed to Anna's husband, J.S. Bach, until scholars corrected this in the 1970s. Petzgold was good-natured and well-regarded amongst his contemporaries.

☐ Perform "Prelude in C Major" for someone or share it with us on our website, www.musicmousestudios.com!

Congratulations, you've completed Lesson 20!

"What you get by achieving your goals is not as important as what you become by achieving your goals."

—ZIG ZIGLAR

LESSON
21
Form and Function

"What is not like the other?" is a common question we teach even kids to recognize. Determining where patterns exist in music is essential in developing efficient practice habits as well as understanding the form of a piece. We will dive more into this in the upcoming lesson!

Warmup Review

☐ Play a C Major Scale with both hands ascending and descending 5 times.

☐ Play a G Major Scale with both hands ascending and descending 5 times.

☐ Play a C Major Arpeggio with both hands.

☐ Play a G Major Arpeggio with both hands.

☐ Play an F Major Arpeggio with both hands.

We will learn the next section of Minuet 3 in G Major. Let's look at the section below and compare it to the section we learned last week.

New section

Last section

Minuet 3
in G Major

Christian Petzgold
Minuet from the "Notebook for Anna Magedalena Bach"

What do you notice? For starters, if we look at the **right hand**, it remains **mostly unchanged** throughout, except for the fi nal two measures of each section. The left hand is also similar, with just the addition of some notes fi lled in here and there.

Referring to the previous section (measures 1-8) as **Section A**, we can label the subsequent section (measures 9-16) as **A'** since it closely resembles A but with slight variations.

It's essential to discern *where* the key differences are between the two sections, which in this case, is primarily found in their endings.

What notes do you see in beats 2 and 3 of measure 8 (using both hands)?

We see D, C, B, and A. The B is a leading note to A, so the core notes here are D, A, and C.

What chord does D, A, and C imply?

If we put these notes into a chord made up of 3rds, we have D, F# (implied), A, and C. This makes a D dominant 7th chord.

☐ Since this piece ends with a V, what cadence is this?

This is called a half cadence, as we learned in previous lessons. Half cadences lack a sense of resolution, like a sentence ending with a question mark that prompts a subsequent response.

☐ Let's look at measure 15. What notes are in this measure?

We see the notes C, D, A, B, G, F#. If we remove the B and G passing tones, we are left with D, F#, A, and C, a D dominant 7th chord.

☐ Let's look at measure 16. What notes are in this measure?

It only has one note, and that is G. This implies a G Major chord, which is also the tonic.

☐ Knowing this, what cadence does the A' section end on (from dominant 7th to tonic)?

The A' section concludes with an authentic cadence, bringing a sense of resolution by ending on the tonic chord. This provides a definitive answer to the question posed in the A section and creates a feeling of finality.

Playing Exercises

Let's practice some legato and staccato exercises before digging into the next section of the piece. Play the exercises below!

Video link: *https://www.musicmousestudios.com/piano-instructional-videos*

☐ Write down all the letters above or below the music notes (this is optional).

☐ How many sharps are in this song, and what is the key signature?

☐ How many beats are there in a measure?

☐ Circle all the staccato notes.

☐ Label the Authentic Cadence at the end of this section with the Roman Numerals (V7 I) under the proper notes.

☐ Clap and count the rhythm of the right hand.

☐ Clap and count the rhythm of the left hand.

☐ Finger the right hand on the table. Follow the fingering provided in the song.

☐ Finger the left hand on the table. Follow the fingering provided in the song.

☐ Finger the song with both hands on the table.

☐ Play this song slowly with your right hand first.

☐ Play this song slowly with your left hand.

☐ Play this song slowly with hands together.

Video link: *https://www.musicmousestudios.com/piano-instructional-videos*

Congratulations, you've completed Lesson 21!

"The only time you should ever look
back is to see how far you've come."

—BTS, SOUTH KOREAN BAND

LESSON
22
Flavor of Flats

Join us as we traverse into the land of flats and explore F Major!

DAY 201

Warmup Review

☐ Play a C Major Scale with both hands ascending and descending 5 times.

☐ Play a G Major Scale with both hands ascending and descending 5 times.

☐ As a review, practice playing the following chord progressions:

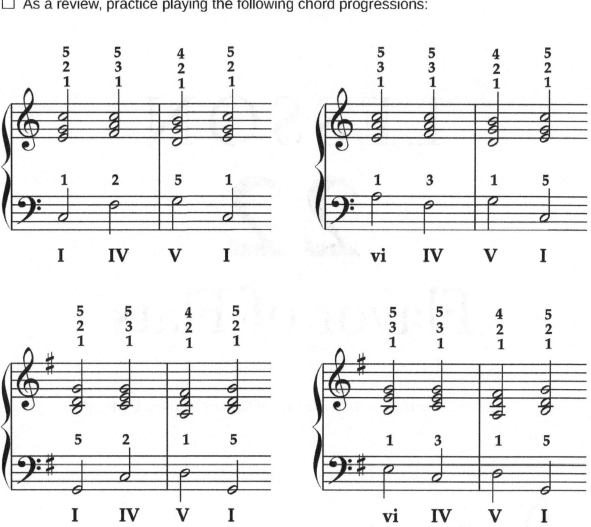

Order of Flats

The Order of Flats serves a similar function to the Order of Sharps - the number of flats present help define the key signature. However, there is one difference to note: the rule does not apply to the first flat, which is B♭. **If a key signature contains only B♭, the key is in F Major.**

The Order of Flats is as follows: B♭, E♭, A♭, D♭, G♭, C♭, F♭. An easy mnemonic to remember this order is the word "BEAD" followed by "GCF" (Greatest Common Factor). Another delightful acronym that can serve as a memory aid is: "Blueberry Eating Always Did Get Cows Fat."

Based on the flats present, **we look at the second-to-last flat to determine the key signature**. For example, if there are 2 flats, B♭ and E♭, we find the second-to-last flat (B♭) and determine that the key is B♭ Major. If there are 3 flats (B♭, E♭, A♭), the second-to-last flat (E♭) indicates that the key is E♭ Major. Similarly, if there are 4 flats (B♭, E♭, A♭, D♭), the second-to-last flat (A♭) reveals that the key is A♭ Major. This method can be used to determine the key signature for the remaining flats in the Order of Flats.

Let's Practice!

See if you can answer the questions below:

1   If a key signature has 2 flats, what are the flats?

2   What key would we be in?

3   If a key signature has 4 flats, what are the flats?

4   What key would we be in?

5   If a key signature has 5 flats, what are the flats?

6   What key would we be in?

7   If a key signature has 7 flats, what are the flats?

8   What key would we be in?

Answers

1   B♭ E♭

2   B♭Major

3   B♭ E♭ A♭ D♭

4   A♭Major

5   B♭ E♭ A♭ D♭ G♭

6   D♭Major

7   B♭ E♭ A♭ D♭ G♭ C♭ F♭

8   C♭Major

F Major Introduction

As a refresher, if a key signature has one flat displayed after the clef, that flat is B♭, and the song is in F Major. This means that every time you see a B in a measure, you will play B♭ instead. This is what an F Major key signature looks like on the staff.

Notice how the B♭ is written on the middle line B in the treble clef. If you remember from previous lessons, the line notes from the bottom to top are EGBDF ("Every Good Boy Does Fine"), with the middle line note being B. This is the B that you want to lower and put a flat on when writing the key signature for F Major.

Similarly, in the bass clef, the line notes from the bottom up are GBDFA ("Good Boys Do Fine Always"). The B line note here is also the one we want to lower in our key signature from B to B♭. For the B♭ in both the treble and bass clef, we want to draw the flat so that the middle portion is on the B line, similar to how you draw a circle for a whole note on line notes.

☐ Draw the F Major key signature above on the staff to your right.

Now, how do we find B♭ on the piano? First, we find B, then we move down to the black note to the left of it.

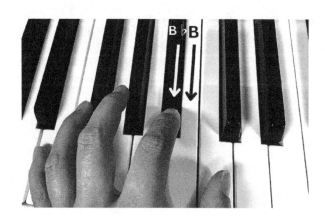

Playing an F Major Scale

Today, we will be learning how to play an F Major scale. As a refresher, a Major scale consists of the half note whole note pattern -

whole whole half
whole
whole whole half

Applying this to the starting note F, we can derive the F Major scale: F, G, A, B♭, C, D, E, F, which is how we conclude that the key signature of F Major consists of 1 flat, and that is B♭.

The image below represents the F Major scale with the corresponding fingerings. In the right hand, we play F with our thumb, G with our index finger, A with our middle finger, and B♭ with our **ring finger**. Then, we cross under with the thumb to play C, followed by D with the index finger, E with the middle finger, and F with the ring finger. When descending, we follow the same pattern but in reverse order. Note that the fingerings differ slightly from C and G Major. Instead of playing fingers 1, 2, 3 and then crossing over with the right thumb, we instead play 1, 2, 3, 4, and then cross the thumb under, due to the B♭.

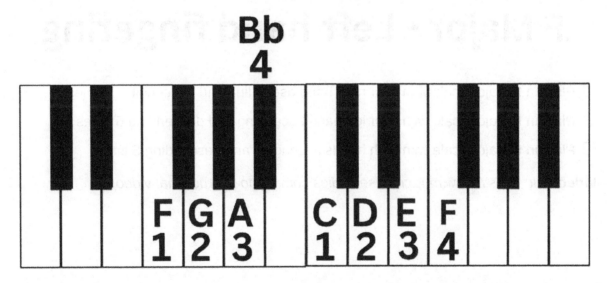

F Major - Right hand fingering

For the left hand, the fingering remains the same as in C and G Major. Please refer to the visual below. With the left hand, we ascend the scale starting with the pinky on F, followed by G with the ring finger, A with the middle finger, B♭ with the index finger, and C with the thumb. Then, we cross over with the middle finger to play D, followed by E with the index finger and F with the thumb. When descending, we start with F on the thumb, go down to E with the index finger, then D with the middle finger, cross under with the thumb to C, and continue descending with B♭ on the index finger, A on the middle finger, G on the ring finger, and finally F on the pinky.

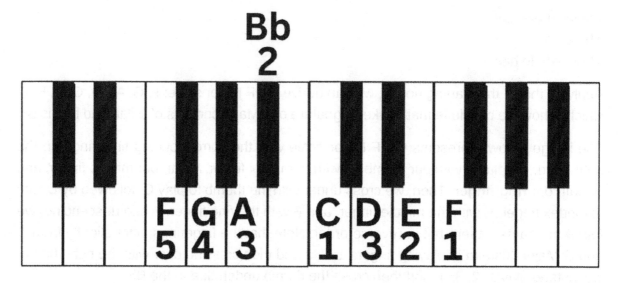

F Major - Left hand fingering

☐ Play an F Major Scale with your right hand ascending and descending 5 times.

☐ Play an F Major Scale with your left hand ascending and descending 5 times.

☐ Play an F Major Scale with both hands ascending and descending 5 times.

Video link: https://www.musicmousestudios.com/piano-instructional-videos

Let's practice some legato and staccato exercises before digging into the next section of the piece. Play the exercises below with the fingerings provided!

Video link: https://www.musicmousestudios.com/piano-instructional-videos

DAY 206
Motifs

Similar to the A sections, we observe a combination of leaps and stepwise motion in this next section of the song. Look at the right hand in beats 2 and 3 in measures 17, 18, and 19. Notice the recurring pattern in the melody, where two 2nd intervals are followed by a leap of a 3rd.

Look at the patterns below -

Despite starting on different notes in each measure, this recurring pattern serves as a melodic anchor for this section, and we call this pattern a **motif**, which is a short musical idea or theme that repeats in different variations throughout a song.

In addition to the motif, if we examine the notes that precede each motif on beat 1 of measures 17, 18, and 19, we find the notes B, A, and G. These descending notes create their own mini melody that accompanies the motif and moves it along the descending scale.

Moving forward, measures 21-22 feature an ascending and then descending scale, followed by leaps in measures 23-24 to conclude this section. This section looks decently different from the previous A sections, so we will call this section B.

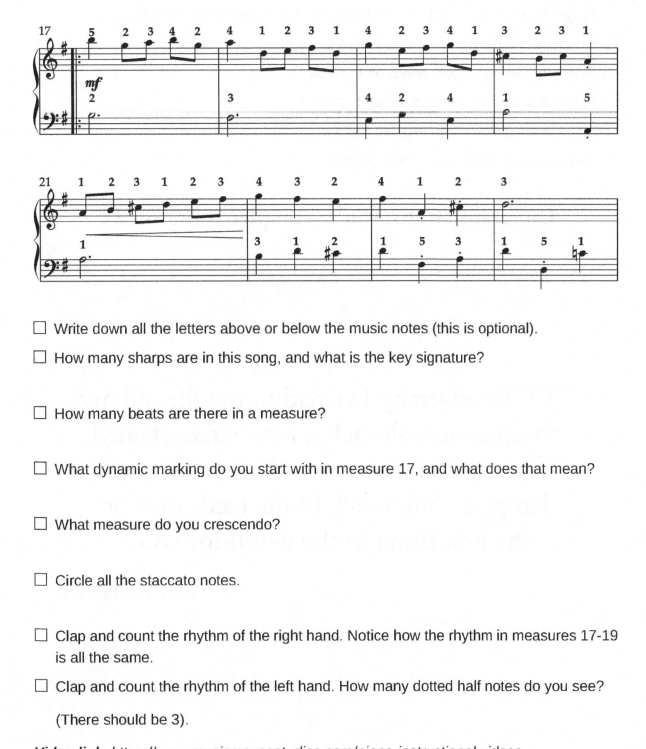

☐ Write down all the letters above or below the music notes (this is optional).

☐ How many sharps are in this song, and what is the key signature?

☐ How many beats are there in a measure?

☐ What dynamic marking do you start with in measure 17, and what does that mean?

☐ What measure do you crescendo?

☐ Circle all the staccato notes.

☐ Clap and count the rhythm of the right hand. Notice how the rhythm in measures 17-19 is all the same.

☐ Clap and count the rhythm of the left hand. How many dotted half notes do you see?

(There should be 3).

Video link: https://www.musicmousestudios.com/piano-instructional-videos

☐ What sharp do you see in measures 20-23?

☐ What symbol do you see in measure 24 in front of the left hand C?

☐ Finger the right hand on the table. Follow the fingering provided in the song.
☐ Finger the left hand on the table. Follow the fingering provided in the song.
☐ Finger the song with both hands on the table.
☐ Play this song slowly with your right hand first.
☐ Play this song slowly with your left hand.
☐ Play this song slowly with hands together.

Congratulations, you've completed Lesson 22!

"All the adversity I've had in my life, all my troubles and obstacles, have strengthened me… You may not realize it when it happens, but a kick in the teeth may be the best thing in the world for you."

—WALT DISNEY

LESSON
23
The Grand Finale

Your remarkable progress as a pianist is truly commendable, showcasing
tremendous growth. We are almost at the finish line! Let's channel that
determination and drive toward a resounding grand finale!!

DAY 211

Warmup Review

☐ Play a C Major Scale with both hands ascending and descending 5 times.

☐ Play a G Major Scale with both hands ascending and descending 5 times.

☐ Play an F Major Scale with both hands ascending and descending 5 times.

☐ As a review, practice playing the following chord progressions:

Let's practice some legato and staccato exercises before digging into the next section of the piece. Play the exercises below with the fingering provided!

Video link: https://www.musicmousestudios.com/piano-instructional-videos

DAY 213

B, B'

In today's lesson, we will cover the final section of this song. Let's compare the previous B section with the new one.

New section

Old section

While this second B section is not as similar to the first B section as the A and A', their melodic structures bear a decent amount of resemblance.

In this new B' section, we observe the usage of a motif on beats 2 and 3 of measures 25-26 in the right hand. Another similarity is found in the last 4 measures of the section, where it once again has a rising and falling scale that is followed by leaps to bring the section to a close.

☐ Look at measure 24. What notes are in that measure, and what chord does that make?

The notes are D and C natural. The implied chord here is a D Dominant 7th chord with D, (F# implied), (A implied), and C natural.

☐ What cadence does section B end on in measure 24?

Because it ends on a V chord, it is a Half Cadence.

Once again, this is similar to the A section ending in a Half Cadence. Let's examine what kind of cadence the B' section ends with.

☐ Look at measure 31, beat 3. What notes do you see there, and what chord does that make?

We see the notes D and F#. This creates a D Major chord (D, F#, and the A is implied). We know that the D is the 5th note in the G Major scale, so D is the dominant.

☐ Look at measure 32. What notes do you see there, and what chord does that make?

The notes we see are G, B, and D. This makes none other than a G Major chord, the tonic in a G Major scale.

☐ What cadence does B' end with?

Knowing that it ends with V I, this is an authentic cadence.

Similar to the transition from A to A', going from a half cadence at the end of B to an authentic cadence in B', this again creates tension and resolution to the tonic.

New Song:
"Minuet 3 in G Major" (Part 4)

☐ Write down all the letters above or below the music notes (this is optional).

☐ How many sharps are in this song, and what is the key signature?

☐ How many beats are there in a measure?

☐ Circle all the staccato notes.

☐ Label the Authentic Cadence at the end of this section with the Roman Numerals (V I) under the proper notes.

☐ What dynamic do you start playing the piece at?

☐ What measure do you crescendo in?

☐ Clap and count the rhythm of the right hand.

☐ Clap and count the rhythm of the left hand.

☐ Finger the right hand on the table. Follow the fingering provided.

☐ Finger the left hand on the table. Follow the fingering provided.

☐ Finger the song with both hands on the table.

☐ Play this song slowly with your right hand first.

☐ Play this song slowly with your left hand.

☐ Play this song slowly with hands together.

Video link: https://www.musicmousestudios.com/piano-instructional-videos

☐ Play a C Major Scale with both hands ascending and descending 3 times.

☐ Play a G Major Scale with both hands ascending and descending 3 times.

☐ Play an F Major Scale with both hands ascending and descending 3 times.

☐ Play a C Major Arpeggio with both hands.

☐ Play a G Major Arpeggio with both hands.

☐ Play an F Major Arpeggio with both hands.

New Song: Minuet 3 in G Major by Christian Petzgold (Part 5)

Minuet 3
in G Major

Christian Petzgold
Minuet from the "Notebook for Anna Magedalena Bach"

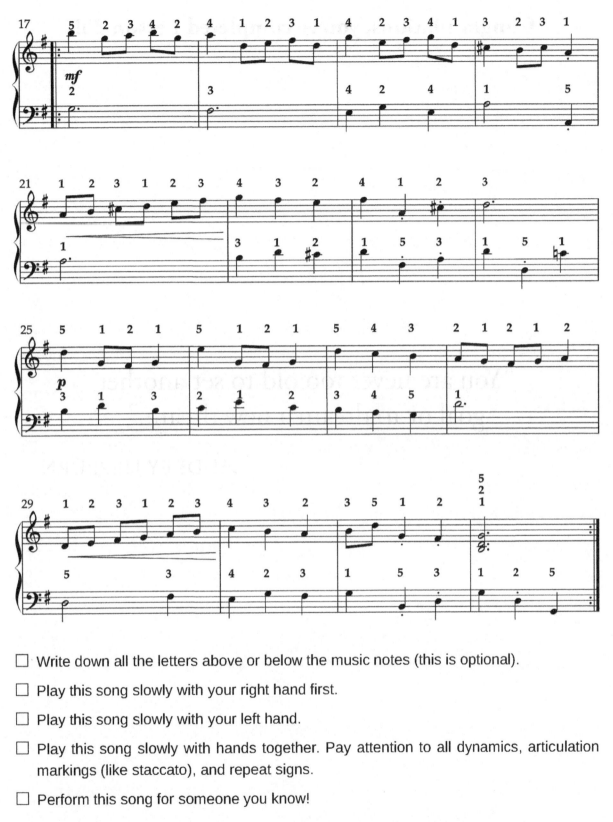

☐ Write down all the letters above or below the music notes (this is optional).

☐ Play this song slowly with your right hand first.

☐ Play this song slowly with your left hand.

☐ Play this song slowly with hands together. Pay attention to all dynamics, articulation markings (like staccato), and repeat signs.

☐ Perform this song for someone you know!

Video link: https://www.musicmousestudios.com/piano-instructional-videos

Congratulations, you've completed Lesson 23!

"You are never too old to set another
goal or to dream a new dream."

—AUDREY HEPBURN

Performance (OPTIONAL)

Practice all of the songs from Book 1 and Book 2 and perform them for someone or share it with us on our website, www.musicmousestudios.com!

- ☐ Mary Had a Little Lamb
- ☐ Down the River
- ☐ Oh When the Saints Go Marching In
- ☐ Twinkle, Twinkle Little Star
- ☐ The Amazing Twinkle, Twinkle Little Star
- ☐ Ode to Joy
- ☐ Go Tell Aunt Rhody
- ☐ Amazing Grace
- ☐ Brahms Lullaby
- ☐ Danny Boy
- ☐ Prelude in C Major
- ☐ Minuet 3

CERTIFICATE
OF AWARD

presented to :

Congratulations! You have graduated from Book 2 -
Your Golden Ears: First Piano Lessons for Adult Beginners!

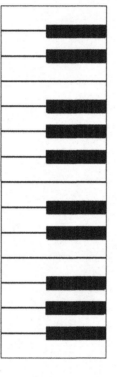

Andrea Chang

Founder of
Music Mouse Studios

Date

Leave A 1-Click Review!

I would be incredibly thankful if you could just take 60 seconds to write a brief review on Amazon, even if it's just a few sentences.

Customer reviews

 5 out of 5

2 global ratings

5 star	████████	100%
4 star		0%
3 star		0%
2 star		0%
1 star		0%

⌄ How customer reviews and ratings work

Review this product

Share your thoughts with other customers

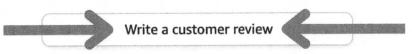

Write a customer review

Conclusion – Beyond the Last Note

Congratulations, you've achieved it! Completing this course was no small accomplishment, but your perseverance has paid off splendidly! Throughout this journey, we've delved into crucial subjects, from honing our finger dexterity through warm-ups, songs, and scales, to exploring music theory at a deeper level through harmonic analysis of cadences and interval movements. You've also learned to elevate your artistry by infusing your playing with expressive techniques, such as dynamics, articulation, and the sustain pedal. You've even conquered intricate compositions like Bach's "Prelude in C Major" and Petzgold's "Minuet 3 in G Major." Furthermore, you've dived into the realm of artistic improvisation, truly creating your own musical path!

As you reach the conclusion of this book, bear in mind that your journey as a pianist is just commencing! Continuing to learn, practice, and challenge yourself is paramount. Don't be discouraged by challenges; instead, see them as stepping stones to growth and improve-ment. You now possess the tools and knowledge to apply what you have learned, and this book will serve as a valuable resource you can always refer back to.

Put into practice all that you have learned and persistently pursue excellence in your piano playing. Embrace the opportunity to apply your knowledge, honing your skills with dedication and a commitment to continuous improvement. We believe in your ability to achieve great-ness in your musical endeavors! Share your progress with us, inspire others, and continue to pursue your musical dreams with passion and determination!!

If you have found value in this book, we kindly ask for your support. Please consider leaving a posi-tive review on Amazon and subscribing to our YouTube channel, where you will find more valuable content and piano lessons! Visit us at https://www.youtube.com/@homeschoolingwithandrea.

For personalized assistance, additional resources, and support, we invite you to explore our website, www.musicmousestudios.com. You will find a wealth of information to aid you on your musical journey.

And don't forget about your free gift!
To receive this exclusive download of additional sheet music and songs, simply visit https://www.musicmousestudios.com/contact and include the text "SHEET MUSIC" in your message.

We have thoroughly enjoyed being a part of your piano journey so far, and we are excited to continue supporting you as you grow and excel as a pianist. The best is yet to come!

Keep playing, keep learning, and keep reaching for the stars!

References

Wikipedia contributors. (2023f). Johannes Brahms. *Wikipedia*. https://en.wikipedia.org/wiki/ Johannes_Brahms

Pew, D. (2018). Classical Music's Most Tragically Romantic Love Triangle — Timpanogos Symphony Orchestra. *Timpanogos Symphony Orchestra*. https://thetso.org/blog/ love-triangle

Songfacts. (n.d.). *Cradle Song by Johannes Brahms - Songfacts*. Songfacts. https://www. songfacts.com/facts/johannes-brahms/cradle-song

Wikipedia contributors. (2022). Christian Petzold (composer). *Wikipedia*. https://en.wikipedia.org/ wiki/Christian_Petzold_(composer)

Christian Petzold: German Composer from The Baroque Era. (n.d.). Galaxy Music Notes. https:// galaxymusicnotes.com/pages/about-christian-petzold

Wikipedia contributors. (2023f). Johann Sebastian Bach. *Wikipedia*. https://en.wikipedia.org/wiki/ Johann_Sebastian_Bach

Simplifying Theory. (2020, June 17). *Supertonic, mediant, submediant and leading-tone | Simplifying Theory*. https://www.simplifyingtheory.com/ supertonic-mediant-submediant-and-leading-tone/

200+ Motivational Quotes To Inspire and Win 2023. (2022, December 1). Shopify. https://www. shopify.com/blog/motivational-quotes

Liles, M. (2023, March 9). Stay Motivated When the Going Gets Tough Thanks to These 100 Quotes About Not Giving Up. Parade: Entertainment, Recipes, Health, Life, Holidays. https://parade.com/980122/marynliles/not-giving-up-quotes/

117 Never Give Up Quotes (+ My 5 Favorite Tips to Help You Keep Going). (2022, April 25). The Positivity Blog. https://www.positivityblog.com/never-give-up-quotes/

Edinburgh, K. (2023). 55 Uplifting Quotes to Encourage Making Progress. Exam Study Expert. https://examstudyexpert.com/ progress-quotes/#quotes-to-help-you-get-a-new-perspective-on-your-progress

You Can Do It Quotes. (n.d.). BrainyQuote. https://www.brainyquote.com/topics/ you-can-do-it-quotes